Praise for *Answering Why*

"This is an amazing book you can apply to every area of your life. Educators, trainers, and anyone working with young people today will discover the tools and strategies to build direction, motivation, and passion in these pages."

—BRIAN TRACY, best-selling author of 86 books

"Mark is fantastic at explaining the pressures and expectations weighing on the younger generation entering the workforce. Written for those looking to hire and retain Generations Y and Z, this book outlines who they are and how we can empower them to turn the business world on its head."

—CHRISTINE HASSLER, generational expert, keynote speaker, best-selling author

"Youth culture today impacts everyone—Gen X and Baby Boomers along with Gen Z and Millennial stakeholders. *Answering Why* will help inform your thinking about how to adjust to an ever-evolving workforce, enabling the reader to create scalable solutions to employee engagement and other workforce opportunities."

—JEFF FROMM, president of FutureCast, keynote speaker, author of *Marketing to Millennials, Millennials with Kids*, and *Marketing to Gen Z*

"Educators have long been searching for a cohesive set of strategies to engage today's young people. In *Answering Why*, Perna delivers it—while making a powerful argument for equipping all students in the K–12 system with both the academic knowledge and technical skill to be competitive, whether college, technical school, or a career is in their immediate future. I'm proud to recommend this book to all parents and educators looking to make a bigger difference for their students!"

—CHRISTY PERRY, superintendent, Salem-Keizer Public Schools

"Engaging. Accurate. Insightful. Mark Perna truly understands how the older and younger generations work (and sometimes don't work) together. His insights will spark productive conversations and challenge the stigmas that have held the younger generations back in today's workforce."

—ADAM ROBINSON, founder and CEO of Hireology,
author of *The Best Team Wins*

"Mark has created a comprehensive playbook full of insight while dispelling the mainstream myths concerning the younger generations. In addition, he strategically creates a compendium for greater conversations as well as a call to action among school administrators, industry leaders, policymakers and higher education providers. This is an essential read for anyone looking to influence education and the greater global economy while lessening the skills gap crisis."

—CYLYNN BRASWELL, executive director of College & Career
Readiness at Northwest Independent School District

"This book will remind educators and workforce development professionals why they care about students and careers. As a member of the Millennial generation, I found the specific examples and real-world success stories compelling. By opening the conversation with useful and practical steps to reach the Why Generation, Mark Perna is working to reframe mindsets about how we connect students to careers. *Answering Why* will be the catalyst to change our thinking about this critical topic."

—JEN SCHOTTKE, vice president in the construction industry,
elected board of education trustee, millennial, and parent

"*Answering Why* is a marvelous tool for workforce development and education organizations across the country. It's an easy read but full of eye-opening insights and actionable steps to connect more effectively with today's up and coming workforce. Parents will also benefit from the strategies to motivate their children to greater performance. Organizations that are looking to build a robust learning and training culture should start with this book. Bravo!"

—JIMMY E. GREENE, president and CEO of ABC Greater Michigan and Greater Michigan Construction Academy

"This is an incredibly important message that will change the face of education and workforce development in this country."

—CATHIE RAYMOND, deputy associate superintendent and state director of Career and Technical Education, Arizona Department of Education

"What an eye-opening book! *Answering Why* reveals the vast potential of today's young people and equips us to answer their why. Mark Perna has created the missing piece in the puzzle of the younger generations that we've been trying to solve blindfolded. This book is going to change the game for students and parents everywhere."

—PAUL GALBENSKI, 2012 Michigan teacher of the year; dean, Oakland Schools

UNLEASHING PASSION,
PURPOSE, *and* PERFORMANCE *in*
YOUNGER GENERATIONS

Answering WhY

Mark C. Perna

GREENLEAF
BOOK GROUP PRESS

Published by Greenleaf Book Group Press
Austin, Texas
www.gbgpress.com

Distributed by Greenleaf Book Group

For ordering information or special discounts for bulk purchases, please contact Greenleaf Book Group at PO Box 91869, Austin, TX 78709, 512.891.6100.

Design and composition by Greenleaf Book Group
Cover design by Greenleaf Book Group
Cover image: ©Shutterstock.com/arka38

Cataloging-in-Publication data is available.

Print ISBN: 978-1-62634-511-9

eBook ISBN: 978-1-62634-512-6

Audiobook ISBN: 978-1-62634-518-8

Part of the Tree Neutral® program, which offsets the number of trees consumed in the production and printing of this book by taking proactive steps, such as planting trees in direct proportion to the number of trees used: www.treeneutral.com

TreeNeutral

Printed in the United States of America on acid-free paper

18 19 20 21 22 23   10 9 8 7 6 5 4 3 2 1

First Edition

Dedication

I was inspired to write *Answering Why* because all around the country, so many people are asking that very question. Why? Why are we struggling to connect meaningfully with those in generations older and younger than our own? Why are our education and workforce development systems broken? Why is the skills gap expanding in our country, and why is there no easy solution in sight?

As a longtime consultant in the related fields of education and workforce development, I believe there is no more urgent moment than now to start solving these challenges facing our nation. Millions of jobs go unfilled in the United States because employers can't find workers with the right skills—and yet millions of people are un- or underemployed. As the industries that drive our economy falter for lack of qualified people, this skills gap will reach crisis proportions. And we can change this when we start answering the essential question of why.

But even more than that, I wrote this book because I see the urgency for employers, parents, and educators to reach the younger generations. I've felt this urgency myself as a father to two amazing young men. I believe we can empower today's younger generations to make a bigger difference than ever before. And if the strategies and stories of the work I do can help generations of young people reach their full potential, then together we've changed the world for the better.

Despite my many mistakes, this book was written for my boys and the world they are helping to create. I love my sons, and I want them to know that they are always the strongest guiding motive for the work I do.

So this work is dedicated to you, Matthew and Nicholas. Thank you for inspiring me to believe in the greatness of your generation.

Contents

Section One: Focus on the Challenge

Chapter One: Closing the Skills Gap 15

Chapter Two: Overcoming Generational Rifts 33

Chapter Three: Getting to Know the Why Generation 45

Section Two: Plan for Exceptional Performance

Chapter Four: Why the Why Generation
Doesn't Hear the Branch Creaking. 67

Chapter Five: Finding the Light at the
End of the Tunnel 85

Chapter Six: Bridging the Awareness Gap 107

Chapter Seven: Building a Competitive Advantage. 139

Section Three: Take Action on the Plan

Chapter Eight: Education with Purpose;
Employment with Passion 163

Chapter Nine: Strategies and Tools to Connect
and Empower 179

Conclusion: The Wade Factor. 199

Acknowledgments 211

Endnotes 213

Index 219

About the Author. 229

Introduction

Did you ever inch out on what looked like a sturdy tree branch only to realize it wasn't as strong as you had thought? You might have just been pushing yourself outside of your comfort zone for some excitement. Little did you know that lurking below the surface of the limb was a crack that would soon broadcast a thunderous creak—and you would face the imminent disaster of plunging downward in a life-threatening fall unless you took action.

In this book I use a creaking-branch metaphor that comes from a childhood experience when I was climbing high in a tree and suddenly heard the branch beneath me start to creak and give way. In that single heart-stopping moment, I learned to do three things: focus, plan, and take action to get to safety.

Focus happens when we experience a serious fear of loss or a sense of urgency, when there is something we desperately want and are in danger of losing. When that happens, we find the ability to laser-focus and prioritize the thing we want, whatever it may be.

Strategic planning follows hard on the heels of focus. This is the stage where we formulate our next steps to alleviate that fear of loss. As human beings we are constantly strategizing, making plans, and solving problems; it is inherent to the way we think and organize our lives.

Action is where we implement our strategic plan by taking the actual steps to put our plan into motion.

Life is not so different from tree climbing. When we're standing out on a limb as we live our lives, when things appear to be going well and on track, hearing a "creak" can announce that something is about to change in a big way. This sense of urgency triggers us to focus on the challenges at hand, strategically plan a new direction, and take action—in fact, dramatic action—to avoid that dangerous plummet.

There is an upside to branch-creak moments. Hearing the branch creak can be an amazingly effective motivational tool. It is during these critical experiences in life that real change is possible because they cause us to focus, plan, and take the necessary action to achieve decisive goals and keep from falling. Growth happens when we step outside our safe space. It rarely happens when we are feeling secure. Hearing a terrifying branch creak in our life is actually a valuable experience because it energizes us to move in a different direction toward a positive result.

Whether you recognize it or not, the branch is creaking in America when it comes to engaging the younger generations and preparing them to successfully enter the workforce. There are some six million open jobs in our country right now—and no one qualified to fill them. We're facing a crisis in both the education system and the arena of workforce development, and it's critical that we focus, plan, and take action before the branch truly breaks.

Let me explain.

The Branch Is Creaking

There is a huge generational shift happening in the United States. The baby boomers, the largest generation ever born in the United States, are retiring, leaving vast numbers of unfilled jobs in many critical economic sectors. As the economy grows into the future, the need for those jobs will only increase—a great opportunity for pretty much anyone currently under the age of 40, right?

Yet the truth is that due to false perceptions, outdated stigmas, and what I like to call the *Awareness Gap*, many of today's young people aren't interested in those open jobs. The six million jobs I'm talking about are middle- to high-skilled, living-wage positions requiring significant training in high-tech environments using state-of-the-art equipment and techniques for fields like advanced manufacturing, construction, healthcare, engineering, aviation, and many others. Sounds pretty cool, doesn't it? Not to many of today's young people. Between false perception and big-picture reality is the Awareness Gap. And the resulting national skills gap crisis in our country is only getting worse. Mark Drury, the vice president of business development with Shapiro & Duncan, Inc., a mechanical engineering and construction company based in Rockville, Maryland, told me that his company can't even chase all the opportunities available to them because they can't find enough qualified people. "We are extremely busy, and the biggest threat we face is not being able to achieve our strategic goals because of the lack of human capital in our industry," Mark said. "We are struggling to find enough qualified employees to tackle what we already have in the pipeline. We can't begin to take on the workload that is currently on the market without adding additional capacity and by increasing the strength of our most important resource—human capital. We have to increase awareness among young people, parents, school systems, and communities about the impressive careers available in this and many other fields."[1]

The lack of interest in these six million open jobs is a paradox since most of the younger generations aren't sufficiently engaged in their current profession. Some 55 percent of young people report feeling unengaged at work.[2] Perhaps even more alarming, some 66 percent expect to leave their current positions by 2020.[3] Two-thirds of the largest working population are planning to leave their current jobs—wow. Alarms should be sounding off everywhere. Why do we have this disconnect?

One answer is that many young people don't want the same kinds of jobs their parents or grandparents had. They aren't as motivated by the safety and security of a good job. Rather, they want a job that has purpose—that means something. They want a job that rewards them with experiences rather than just money, even as their college loan balances balloon. (At last count, some 42 million Americans currently have student loans, with more than 5 million at least 90 days behind on payments.[4]) And they also want to know why a work process or activity is important. Why should they do it this way or that way? Why is a particular step important in the grand scheme of things? This inquisitive nature started at birth and has been nurtured, praised, and stimulated throughout their lives. It should come as no surprise that younger generations want things explained, spelled out, and clear—that is exactly how we reared them. That's why I've come up with a new name for today's young people to help frame this challenge: *the Why Generation.*

The Why Generation encompasses both Generation Y (the millennials) and Generation Z (currently the youngest generation). These cohorts approach education, careers, and everything else in their lives with a strong desire to understand the purpose behind what they do. "Because I said so" is not enough of a reason anymore, and we feel this shift in the classroom dynamic, in workplace interactions, and in every conversation we have with today's young people. The Why Generation asks a serious question. Do we have the answer?

There's another side to all this inquisitiveness. In their quest for purpose and meaning, young people today wind up job-hopping in search of the perfect fit, which creates friction and even resentment among those trying to fill those jobs. Today's managers and educators, who come from every generation, now label young people as entitled, unfocused, and even lazy. (Some young people even say that about themselves!) They ask why young people act this way. Why can't they be more like us? Add it all up, and you have a lot of people urgently asking why we're experiencing these problems and how we can better connect with and unlock the potential of tomorrow's workforce. We're having a national branch-creak moment.

We have some 100 million talented members of the Why Generation seeking reasons and purpose and another 220 million people in older generations struggling to provide reasons and purpose. We need to find those answers. Our nation is increasingly suffering from the aptly named skills gap I mentioned earlier. Millions of jobs in sectors crucially important to our economy and society are open, and we have no one with the right skills—or even the desire—to fill them.

Are we sure we are truly preparing the Why Generation for the opportunities ahead? What help can we provide them in the classroom and beyond in terms of education and workforce development? Do we need a better approach?

The branch is creaking. Time to focus, plan, and take action. Now is the time to embrace meaningful strategies to empower and engage the young people of the Why Generation and help them fulfill their vast potential.

Why I Hear the Branch Creaking

I am the founder of a company called TFS, which works with businesses and schools across the nation to help them attract and retain significantly more of the right employees or students, in the right positions or programs, for the right reasons. I am also the father of two members of the Why Generation, my sons Matt and Nick, who have provided me with plenty of experiences and stories to share as I travel North America delivering keynote speeches and coaching my clients. My message is all about how to recruit, retain, and motivate what I believe to be one of the greatest generations—yes, today's young people—to greater performance in their educational programs and careers.

At TFS, we work with employers, universities, community and technical colleges, career centers, unified and comprehensive school districts, and many statewide and international educational organizations to help improve performance with the Why Generation. Our overarching mission is to share and support our clients' passion for making a difference.

To that end, I collaborate with a talented group of professionals who share a common vision for changing the education and workforce development sectors for the better. I am extremely proud of the work we do and the impact we are making nationwide. It's a much-needed service we provide. In my travels, I constantly hear these questions:

- What can we do to reach today's young people and motivate them to higher performance in their careers and all other areas of life?

- Why do the younger generations act the way they do?

- How can we overcome generational differences in the workplace?

- Why do we need to change the educational and workforce development paradigm in the United States?

- How can we improve employee retention and performance?

- Why is our national skills gap expanding, and how can we close it?

Differences in worldviews, habits, perspectives, and values between generations—or as I call them, *Generational Rifts*—are nothing new. But what is new is the alarming rate at which our country's skills gap and college debt burden are expanding. While many factors are at play in this national crisis, many experts believe that the radical differences between today's younger and older generations are among the most significant causes. Yet looking at it solely as a generational issue misses the key point.

What worked in the past to educate and train young people isn't working anymore. Business and industry's desperation for skilled workers has its roots in our educational system and even in our parenting.

We face a national epidemic of rising college costs, decreasing degree-requiring jobs, and employer frustration with the younger generations in the workplace. Yet we continue to rely on an outdated educational and workforce training system that was developed 50 years ago. Declining educational funding is another huge challenge for schools—another branch creak—as they are being forced to do more with less each year. The critical topic of career development has been drastically cut or even eliminated in many cases. And yet we're puzzled about why our young people are underemployed.

Young people have changed, and we need to change how we connect with them. The question shouldn't be just about getting young people ready for college. Rather, it should be about preparing them for careers for which college is one of many available options. I'm a huge fan of going to college if the career you want to pursue requires a degree. But contrary to what many young people today are told, going to college is not the only means to a successful career and lifestyle. To have a great career and life, you can certainly pursue a

PhD. But you can also get a two-year degree, earn a certification, acquire a license, or complete an apprenticeship. That's not a message our young people hear anymore—and that needs to change. In short, what got us here won't get us where we need to go. We need to change course if we are truly interested in unlocking the full potential of the coming generations.

The members of the Why Generation have immense potential to change the world for the better. And they want to do just that. They're tenacious and talented, and when they find a cause they believe in, they give it everything they have. Yes, they're different from older generations. But might that be a good thing? If we adjusted our viewpoint a bit, couldn't we begin to see their perceived weaknesses as strengths instead? What if we began to think of this moment in our history as a branch-creak opportunity to rethink our approach to education and workforce development?

After all, responsibility for the future of our great nation currently lies with our largest generation, the baby boomers. I think we can all agree that we want our kids and young people to strive for maximum performance in every area of their lives (motivated by their own unique interests, talents, and abilities). Our schools and communities have a big role to play in that goal. We also want Why Generation workers to help shrink the skills gap for employers, clients, and shareholders because our national economy hangs in the balance. It's clear that we need to make major changes on a national scale to achieve these goals. The good news is that we've done things like this before.

When Our National Branch Creaks

Americans have experienced countless events that have caused our collective branch to creak. Each instance forced us to focus, plan, and take action—sometimes massive action on a national scale. Today our growing skills gap, misaligned education system, and college debt epidemic are creating yet another branch-creak opportunity for our nation to step up and overcome the difficulties standing in our way.

World War II is an example of a national crisis that motivated an entire generation to rise to the challenge and make tremendous sacrifices to protect the United States and our allies. The actions of those Americans, both in battle and at home, inspired author and former NBC anchor Tom Brokaw to label them the greatest generation. This generation also overcame the ravages of the Depression and is largely responsible for making the United States a global superpower. And they did it by having a shared purpose, a shared responsibility, and a shared vision sparked by a national branch creak.

Another national branch creak came in the wake of October 4, 1957, when the Soviet Union launched *Sputnik*, a 23-inch-diameter radio pulse satellite that achieved low Earth orbit lasting 92 days and 1,440 orbits. It was visible worldwide and its radio pulse signals could be heard from Earth. In America, the launch created fear that the Soviets could one day dominate space flight to increase spying capabilities and perhaps launch weapons proficiently from a tactical space platform in orbit above the United States.

This realization—or branch creak—caused a powerful fear of loss and sense of urgency to beat the Soviets in the domination of space, which naturally became the next frontier. It accelerated the rising tensions of the Cold War and created the Space Race, culminating in the July 20, 1969, landing of *Apollo 11* on the surface of the moon. The focus, planning, and action that followed *Sputnik's* historic voyage changed our world forever and spurred decades of high-tech innovations unparalleled in history. We owe much of our sophisticated technology today to the advancements that took place during the 1957 branch creak that fueled the Space Race.

As I think of these events, I'm reminded of Homer Hickam, whose life was the basis for the movie *October Sky*. As a teenager growing up in Coalwood, West Virginia, Homer was inspired to build his own rocket after seeing *Sputnik* magically sail across the night sky. If he was successful in building and testing a homemade rocket—no small feat—he could enter it in a state science competition and possibly receive a college scholarship, which would mean his escape from a life spent working in the coal mines. I remember one scene in particular that beautifully illustrates the personal branch creak in his life and how the "want-to" created the "how-to" for him to achieve this goal (a concept we'll explore further). Eagerly questioned about his chances of entering the science competition, Homer's teacher Miss Riley says, "Well, maybe it's not for you." "Well, what do you mean?" he asks. "Homer, you got a great mind. But science requires math . . . which has never been one of your favorite subjects." His response: "I'll learn the math, I'll do whatever it takes." And he does.

Homer Hickam went on to build his rocket, win the science competition, go to college, and become a NASA engineer. When faced with a branch creak that brought a fear of loss and sense of urgency, he found a way to overcome the obstacles and make his dreams a reality.

Sputnik changed everything—for individuals like Homer Hickam and for our country as a whole. What was initially seen as a significant challenge to our way of life in fact spurred the action that led to the astonishing success and advancement we have enjoyed in space exploration and discovery.

As Homer Hickam and our entire nation learned, hearing the branch creak is not something to be feared. On the contrary, it is something to be embraced as a significant opportunity to focus, plan, and take the necessary action that may change the course of history, as it did in the Space Race throughout the 1960s.

In other words, if we want to overcome our current national

branch creak, it's time for us to focus, plan, and take action. It's time to unleash the power of younger generations to achieve the performance and success they are capable of—in every area of their lives. And it's time to show them why.

What's Next

As a way to help you understand the challenge we face in connecting with and unleashing the full potential of the Why Generation, I've divided this book into three sections:

SECTION ONE: FOCUS ON THE CHALLENGE

In this first section, we'll talk about why the skills gap exists—and continues to grow wider—and how we need to overcome our biases and misconceptions about young people to help close it. We'll also discuss who the members of the Why Generation are and why they think and act the way they do as a way to understand their strengths, as well as their weaknesses.

- Chapter One: Closing the Skills Gap
- Chapter Two: Overcoming Generational Rifts
- Chapter Three: Getting to Know the Why Generation

SECTION TWO: PLAN FOR EXCEPTIONAL PERFORMANCE

Once we know who the young people of the Why Generation are, we'll dig into why they are missing the massive opportunity before them. We'll also discuss key tools that I use to help young people rethink what they want from their lives and careers.

- Chapter Four: Why the Why Generation Doesn't Hear the Branch Creaking

- Chapter Five: Finding the Light at the End of the Tunnel

- Chapter Six: Bridging the Awareness Gap

- Chapter Seven: Building a Competitive Advantage

SECTION THREE: TAKE ACTION ON THE PLAN

Our current educational and workforce development system is broken because it doesn't connect learning with a larger purpose for young people today. But we can change that. I offer some advice and tips educators, employers, and even parents can use to unlock the full potential of the Why Generation.

- Chapter Eight: Education with Purpose; Employment with Passion

- Chapter Nine: Strategies and Tools to Connect and Empower

CONCLUSION: THE WADE FACTOR

I will wrap up the book on an inspirational note by showing what can happen when we implement the key points I've shared throughout the book. These principles are producing results for teachers, administrators, parents, employers, managers, and many others around the country. And now they can help transform your paradigm.

Are you ready? Let's step out on a limb together.

Focus on the Challenge

CHAPTER ONE

Closing the Skills Gap

A few years ago, when I was invited to speak at a Pathways to Prosperity workforce development conference at Harvard University, I discovered a piece of the answer to why there are millions of unfilled positions in the United States alongside millions of people seeking employment. The invitation-only conference focused on closing America's expanding gap between what skills employers need and what skills employees possess. Attendees at the conference included high-level statewide education teams of K–12 superintendents, chancellors of community college systems, business and industry executives from Fortune 100 companies, and Departments of Education and Labor personnel. About 400 individuals were invited, but over 600 showed up—an indication of the tremendous concern that business and education leaders are experiencing over this issue. For them, the branch is creaking loudly and clearly.

The reason for the conference was simple: employers are becoming desperate for a skilled workforce that possesses the hard and soft skills needed to thrive in their businesses. Hard skills are those actual hands-on skills needed to do the job, while soft skills (or the phrase I use in this book and in my work as a term of art, *Professional Skills*) are necessary life and people skills—communicating properly, showing up on time, working a full day, problem solving, taking on leadership roles, and many others. As I've stated earlier, there are millions of people in America who are out of work, and there are also millions of jobs that go unfilled in this country because of a lack of skilled workers. This is the ever-expanding skills gap. It is occurring because our culture has such a long-established love affair with going to college that we are doubling down as a nation to get more and more people into college even though college is not delivering those critical hard skills and Professional Skills needed to make our economy work.

According to a recent study from Georgetown University's Center on Education and the Workforce, by 2025 the United States will be short 11 million certificate holders and degree holders to support the economy.[1] Getting their students into college is currently the main focus of almost every high school in America— as if mere college attendance is the ultimate goal. But so many college students fail to finish the degree they set out to achieve. Not only that, but the job market today is no longer built solely on college-degreed positions. As technology evolves, workers with specialized industry certifications and licenses are in greater demand than ever.

That's a message that is near and dear to Dr. Kevin Fleming, a scholar, speaker, and entrepreneur who is the creative force behind the wildly popular video entitled "Success in the New Economy." "We have an oversaturation of people with degrees but who also have no tangible skills," Kevin told me. "And I speak from personal experience as someone who is well educated but who didn't have the skills to do anything."[2] In his video, Kevin frames this paradox this way:

The true ratio of jobs in our economy is 1:2:7. For every occupation that requires a master's degree or more, two professional jobs require a university degree, and there are over half a dozen jobs requiring a one-year certificate or two-year degree; and each of these technicians are in very high-skilled areas that are in great demand. This ratio is fundamental to all industries. It was the same in 1950, the same in 1990, and will be the same in 2030. The hope for encouraging university education is that as the number of university-trained workers increases, the demand for their services in the workplace will increase as well. Unfortunately, this is not so. The whole pie may get bigger as the labor force and the economy grows, but the ratio will not change. The reality is there will not be more professional jobs available within the labor market. And some professional jobs have been replaced by technology, or are being outsourced.[3]

While Kevin says he didn't invent the 1:2:7 ratio, he describes it as brilliant in its simplicity and ability to communicate the problems we are creating by pushing young people to obtain degrees while simultaneously ignoring the importance of also acquiring valuable work skills. Kevin points to one example where, during the Occupy Wall Street protests that occurred around the country in 2009, the national news featured one young person who wanted the government to forgive the student loans he had taken out to pursue a master's degree in puppetry. "He was angry because he couldn't get a job," Kevin told me. "I admire him for pursuing his dream. But should we really expect the government to subsidize his degree? I think the bigger point is how crucial it is for our students and their parents to become smarter consumers of education."

We need to change the expectation and educational paradigm in America that college is the only career pathway promoted to our young people. It's not that Kevin and I are against college. The point is that college for all is not the answer to our pressing skills gap crisis. There are many high-paying, high-skilled careers that require a specialized industry credential or certification, not a college degree. As a nation, we need to help students discover what they love to do and how to achieve their dream—whatever that dream is.

To accomplish this we must prioritize career development exploration and education as an integral part of the K–12 system. Higher education is remarkably expensive, and yet many students head off to college without a clear plan of what they would like to do with their lives. The year 2016 was the 18th consecutive year in which Americans' education debt rose. No other form of household debt has increased at this rate.

As I've said, I am a huge fan of going to college. I did it myself. The Awareness Gap that we battle today is the assumption that college is the only path a young person can take to create a successful life. In addition, we don't do a good enough job of informing our young people about the pitfalls they may face when they go to college. We should want them to choose college as a clearly defined step toward their career attainment—not because everyone else is going, not because they think they cannot succeed without a degree, and not because they view college as the place where they figure out their life direction. College is a great postsecondary option—if your career path requires it. Too many people today go just to go—often failing to finish their course of study, missing out on profitable career paths that require specialized postsecondary but not university training, and increasing our nation's student-loan default rate.

One of the central questions discussed at the Harvard conference I attended was this: how do we move the country away from the belief that everyone has to go to a four-year university to be a successful and productive citizen? (Yes, it's ironic that this urgent question was being addressed in a university setting.) As I've said, getting their students into college is currently a primary goal of almost every high school in the United States—as if college admission itself is the goal. And this trend only seems to be growing: 81 percent of the younger members of the Why Generation believe a college education is necessary for a good career,[4] and it is estimated that one in two of them will become university educated.[5] For context, just 25 percent of Gen Xers, the generation preceding the millennials, have a college degree.[6] As part of my remarks that day at Harvard, I talked about the phrase *college and career ready* that has taken hold nationwide. The challenge I see with this statement is that no one notices the word *and* between the words *college* and *career.* It is really understood as *college career ready*—as if college is always the first step in becoming career ready.

I believe we have missed the point. Shouldn't the ultimate goal be to prepare all students to be career ready? We have put our focus in the wrong place. Instead, preparing all students to be career ready should mean that students choosing a career requiring a four-year university degree should attend a four-year baccalaureate program. Students interested in a career requiring a two-year associate degree should take that path. Students wanting to pursue a career in any other area should work toward the certifications, licensures, and apprenticeships needed to succeed in their chosen field. Lots of training options are available, so let students choose the direction and follow the pathway needed to achieve their "want-to" goals in life. It seems like common sense, doesn't it?

"We decided that every kid needed to fit a cookie-cutter mold and that they needed to go to university," says Michelle Martinez, a lifelong public school teacher. "If you talk to any parent, what they want for their kid is to go to college and get a good job. That's the message we sold them. But as public educators, we need to reteach the message that there are other options available. We need to show kids their expanded opportunities."[7]

There must also be a living-wage job or career waiting for a young person at the end of that pathway—regardless of the pathway they have chosen. For example, far too many students finish a degree and only then discover that they can't get a job in that field (like the young man mentioned earlier who attained a master's degree in puppetry). They need to understand that simply picking a career direction, college, or any other option isn't enough; the outcome must be viable and sustainable—especially if they acquire significant debt along the way.

To remedy this Awareness Gap, we need to prioritize career development exploration and education as part of the K–12 system. The rising cost of higher education has become crippling to many families and young people today. Despite the cost, we continue to urge students to go to college, even if they don't have a clear idea of what discipline and career field they want to pursue. "We do career exploration at the highest dollar amount possible, and it's called university," says Paul Galbenski, a Teacher of the Year in the state of Michigan who now runs an Oakland County Public Schools technical campus outside of Detroit. "And there's no guarantee attached to getting a degree. The result is that today's young people face crushing debt."[8]

What's more, the number of college students who actually complete their degree is remarkably poor in the United States—by some reports, as low as 50 percent.[9] Some industry experts believe that figure may be far lower. We have taught young people that their ultimate goal is to get into college rather than make the most of their time in school.

It's like when you watch the 100-meter dash at the Olympics. Men and women have trained for years, maybe even most of their lives, for this one moment. With the crack of the gun they're off, running as fast as they can until they cross the tape. Most runners then begin to slow gradually to a walk down the track, their energy expending. But some runners give it everything they have just as they cross the finish line and crumple into a heap on the ground, completely spent. I think our young people today approach getting into college the second way: once they cross the finish line, they stop cold because they think they have completed their goal. They don't keep training for what comes next.

And the challenges don't end there. More than 50 percent of the people who do complete their degree are either unemployed or significantly underemployed; that is, they are not making a wage commensurate with their education.[10] These students either chose a field of study where no jobs were available or they didn't develop the Professional Skills they needed to land a job of their choice. This is a wakeup call. Simply pushing more students into college is not the answer to closing the skills gap or solving the critical needs of business and industry in America. According to Galbenski, "We've been on this message of sending kids to college for so long that we have gutted the career programs that used to exist in middle school. Kids today just don't know what other paths might be available to them. We need to get back to the point where everyone has a chance to see what options are available—which are limitless."

Another damaging aspect of the college-only mindset is the outcome for young people who aren't ready or able to go to college after high school. What happens to them? That's a question that Jimmy Greene, the CEO of Associated Builders and Contractors, Greater Michigan Chapter, is asking. As someone whose job it is to advocate for skilled trade jobs, Greene admittedly walks a fine line: "I'm never trying to discourage kids from going to college, but when we have the entire education system pushing kids to university and community college, they're forgetting something. While they might be celebrating the fact that 60 percent of their kids go on to college, what happens to the other 40 percent? We have somehow forgotten them."[11]

Greene knows it wasn't bad intent that caused the system to overlook the kids not headed to college, especially in rural and inner-city areas where college is not the norm for many families. But what opportunities are those students being given to become productive citizens and taxpayers? Do they even know there are great, living-wage careers they can pursue that don't require them to go to college? Can't we arm these young people with real skills earlier in life so they can succeed whether they go to college or not? If we don't, how can we expect them to land meaningful employment? "The skills gap was bound to happen," says Greene. "How could it not have?"

Eye-Opening Insights from Fortune 100 Executives

Over lunch at the Harvard conference, I sat at a round table with four Fortune 100 senior executives. Two were from advanced manufacturers, one represented an agricultural company, and another was from the computer industry. (It just so happened that a U.S. Assistant Secretary of Education and a U.S. Assistant Secretary of Labor were also sitting at the table.) We had a dynamic conversation about building a skilled and well-trained workforce in America. The group asked a lot of questions about how I help schools across the country enroll and retain more of the right students, in the right programs, for the right reasons. They were fascinated that there was a company focused on increasing graduation rates with career-focused students and were quick to note the similarities between what I am able to accomplish with my clients and what they are trying to accomplish on national and global scales. In essence, they are trying to do the same thing: recruit and retain more of the right employees, in the right positions, for the right reasons. This quickly became our common ground and the foundation for a remarkably interesting dialogue.

As we discussed the growing skills gap in the United States, one of the manufacturing executives mentioned an anticipated company hire of 15,000 to 20,000 employees over the coming 24 to 36 months. This company is a high-tech global manufacturer with facilities worldwide. Manufacturing, the executive told us, is different today than it was many years ago. Their facilities are the cleanest, brightest, most sophisticated, advanced manufacturing sites you can imagine. He said you can eat off the floor of any of their plants—literally. He went on to say that the advanced equipment and modern facilities were something to see, far different than what people envision. These were high-tech, high-skilled, and high-wage jobs in these advanced manufacturing plants.

He then explained how the workforce has changed over the past five years—not even a decade or two. Just five years ago, there were three distinct groups of labor his company would hire: high skilled, medium skilled, and low skilled. As few as five years ago, low-skilled laborers and support personnel made up a significant portion of the workforce. Today that percentage has dwindled to almost nothing due to the expanded use of advanced technology, robotics, and streamlined manufacturing processes, all of which are necessary to compete in a global marketplace. It is the high-skilled and medium-skilled jobs that they need to fill in order to stay competitive. As a result, there is less and less opportunity for low-skilled workers.

This executive then looked across the table and put both hands out directly in front of him, as if showing us the size of a fish he had caught. His palms were roughly two feet apart as he said, "Mark, this is the entire spectrum of the 15,000 to 20,000 people we have to hire over the next 24 to 36 months. Do you know how many of these people need a college degree?" I thought for a moment and said, "I don't know." He then slapped his hands together—which really grabbed my attention—and then edged his hands apart until they were almost touching, with only a sliver of space between them. "This many. Mark, we need the rest of this entire spectrum to accomplish our goals. We need high-skilled individuals we can train to operate, calibrate, and maintain many hundreds of millions of dollars' worth of equipment." In his view, the unfortunate place at which we find ourselves is that we as a society view those who go to a four-year university as high achievers, and we view those who attend a career center, a vocational training program, or a community or technical college as being somehow lesser. Yet our workforce is starving for people who have developed the hands-on skills, work history, and experiences that come with certifications, apprenticeships, licensures, and career training programs—not necessarily just college. A degree may not be nearly enough on its own, without a skill or experience, to land someone a job anymore. This point was then echoed by each of the other executives at the lunch.

If only a sliver of these 20,000 new workers require a college degree to land a highly desirable job, why is it the goal of almost every high school in America to graduate their students and send them off to college? Why does the vast majority of the Why Generation think a college education is absolutely essential to a good career?

We had discussed this at the table for a few moments when another executive of an advanced manufacturing and engineering company added the following insight. He said that his company made a strategic decision 10 years ago to no longer hire people with a master's degree. I stared at him in questioning disbelief. This was a huge, household-name, high-tech global manufacturer and advanced engineering firm. "What do you mean?" I asked. He went on to explain that they no longer hire people with education for education's sake. They *only* hire people based on their work history and experience. My eyes widened even more when he said, "Now, if you have a good work history and the experiences necessary to thrive in any position we are hiring for, including the CEO—and you happen to have a master's degree—the master's degree won't hurt you." Yes, he actually said, "The master's degree won't hurt you." Where my jaw dropped in the discussion was when each of the other company executives at the table echoed that exact same strategy related to hiring people with a master's degree. They had been doing it for different lengths of time, but all shared that common strategy.

I found it remarkably telling that a company would make this strategic decision. After much thought, I understood it. Education is not work history or experience; it is simply education. Until you have the relevant skills, work history, and experiences that demonstrate your grasp and use of the knowledge, then you simply have what my father called book smarts. I found this entire discussion fascinating because it showed how large, successful corporations view the changing workforce in this country based on their individual need to compete globally.

Throughout my work with comprehensive and unified school districts, career schools, and technical and community colleges, I have seen an abundance of career fields that are totally dismissed by students today because they simply do not understand the high-income potential of those fields. It's the Awareness Gap in action. A job such as precision machinist is the high-skilled and high-wage type of job that my lunchmates and I were discussing. Manufacturers around the country are in desperate need of precision machinists, but attracting the younger generations to the work is remarkably difficult. Several reasons probably account for the lack of interest: the work looks hard and dirty; insufficient career development in middle and high schools creates a lack of understanding about these opportunities; such programs are incorrectly perceived as boring and unfulfilling; and there is a stigma that only lower-performing students choose these kinds of career fields. Yet these fields deliver immediate employment, high wages, advancement opportunities, and job security because there are simply not enough skilled workers out there. They also deliver an advantageous pathway to college and many other additional opportunities. We have a real opportunity to rediscover these forgotten career paths and make them cool again in a way that Mike Rowe, the star of the TV show *Dirty Jobs*, has tried to do. In fact, Rowe has become a vocal advocate for the skilled trades and for finding ways to steer more young people into them to shrink the skills gap we face as a nation. "The opportunities are all over the place," he says. "The jobs that exist right now don't require four years of liberal arts study. They require the willingness to learn a skill that's actually in demand."[12]

Consider, for example, that in the state of Pennsylvania alone, there is already a shortage of some 90,000 construction workers. But the state is also in the middle of a building and energy boom, and billions of dollars of spending are budgeted for the next few years. And Pennsylvania is far from alone—employers across the nation who rely on skilled workers simply cannot find qualified people to drive these industries forward.

Another example comes from an executive I met who works for a firm in Ohio that makes complex parts and components for the aerospace industry. This executive told me that one of their biggest challenges in hiring young people is they can't get enough candidates to pass a drug test. Marijuana is now legal to purchase and consume in some states, but the company has a zero-tolerance policy, and too many candidates, believing that since it's legal in some places they don't have to worry about it anywhere, fail when they apply for a job there. In fact, the company has started giving drug tests at the time of application because far too many candidates were moving all the way through the interview process only to fail the drug test. The nationwide prevalence of drugs is increasing the skills gap and driving workforce development concerns to a new level. This company has been having such a hard time filling positions that it's been forced to import people from abroad to take these high-paying jobs. We're facing a crisis that goes beyond traditional trade industries as well, with sectors like healthcare, biotechnology, and information technology begging for skilled workers who meet company standards to fill positions. But where are those workers going to come from? Talk about a branch creak.

Jimmy Greene from Associated Builders and Contractors in Michigan, whom I quoted earlier, is working to address exactly this issue by opening training centers for young people to help fill the positions his member organizations so desperately need to fill. It's worth noting that not only are the graduates of these career and technical education programs (CTE for short) moving toward meaningful employment, they are also fulfilling their potential as productive, intelligent, and stable citizens.

If the term CTE conjures up images of grubby tools and shop class for you, consider that today's CTE is a far cry from the vocational education of the past. Driven by technology and centering on high-paying, in-demand career fields, CTE is the unsung hero of a fully rounded high school education. These career and technical programs awaken the passion for achievement through hands-on experiences that capture the imagination of our young people. CTE involvement is also highly relevant to academics: CTE students who are exposed to career options early on in their educational journey graduate high school in greater numbers (93 percent, over the national average of 80 percent) and report higher levels of engagement in the learning process.[13] Career and technical programs also provide embedded (applied) academics that, when combined with powerful technical skills, give students a distinct competitive advantage.

That's why, contrary to popular opinion, early career exploration expands rather than limits a student's opportunities. Say a student completes a career-tech program in high school. She can now:

1. go to college while using her career-tech skills to earn a higher wage to pay for her education and living expenses;

2. pursue advanced postsecondary training in her chosen field; or

3. jump right into her career and start working her way up.

CTE is not about making one choice for the rest of your life; rather, it's a gateway to more and better choices and opportunities. As Greene puts it, "Our obligation as a society is to help expand the number of options and opportunities for young people. The question is, which buffet are they picking from? Our goal is not to build better-skilled tradespeople. We are building better well-rounded people who have skills. They also have an ambition and a destination in mind, and we can show them how to get there."

Consider the story of a student I met named Sidney, who attended a CTE school in rural Arizona in addition to her regular high school classes. Sidney was a standout in her class, and she knew from a young age what she wanted to do in life: to become a medical assistant. To get to that destination, she had set a goal of attending the University of Arizona, where she could earn the degree that would open up that career for her.

But Sidney was also learning real skills in her career and technical program. She knew how to take someone's vital signs and blood pressure, for example, as well as how to administer an EKG. Sidney had also developed impressive communication skills—part of those Professional Skills I mentioned earlier—that enabled her to make a patient feel at ease as she tested them.

Those skills also helped Sidney land an after-school internship at a medical clinic. I later learned that the folks running that clinic were so impressed with Sidney's skills and bedside manner that, when she graduated and was getting ready for college, they made her an offer: they wanted to hire her full time instead. She already had the skills they were looking for. Even better, they offered to foot her tuition bill so she could go to college part time. In other words, Sidney found a way to earn a great wage while she learns. Who knows what Sidney might decide to do in the future with her proven skills and undergraduate degree? One thing is for sure: she won't have any college debt, and her eyes will be open about her future potential. Don't you think that's a story we could all be inspired by?

The takeaway here is that we can generate exceptional performance by helping our young people achieve satisfying careers in a multitude of fields by understanding their generational traits, how they think, and what motivates them to make decisions. We also need to overcome our own biases of how we think young people should act and approach their careers—which is a subject we'll turn to next.

CHAPTER ONE INSIGHTS

- The United States faces a severe skills gap where there simply aren't enough workers armed with the right skills and education to keep the economy moving forward.

- At the same time, more and more students are graduating from college without the skills they need, coupled with the fact that they now have to deal with crippling debt. We have turned college into an expensive career exploration program.

- The 1:2:7 ratio states that for every occupation that requires a master's degree or more, two professional jobs require a university degree, and over half a dozen jobs require a one-year certificate or two-year degree. This holds true across all industries.

- U.S. employers have shifted their hiring goals to prioritize candidates with real work experience rather than academic knowledge alone.

- Because of this, there should be a massive shift in how we think about preparing our young people. We should no longer be trying to put them on a path to "college and career readiness." We need to simplify our message to make young people truly career ready by allowing them to take whatever path they need to reach their goals based on their own unique interests, talents, and abilities.

- One of the ways we can close the skills gap facing the country is to make career-minded education cool again. These programs aren't just for the kids who aren't on the path to university; they should be presented as viable opportunities for every young person to gain a competitive advantage.

- Contrary to popular opinion, early career exploration in middle and high school expands rather than limits a student's opportunities.

CHAPTER TWO

Overcoming Generational Rifts

No matter whom you talk to across the country, it has become clear that the older generations think the younger generations are missing the boat. At the same time, the younger generations think the older generations missed the boat. Obviously, the world has changed significantly in the last several decades. While there have always been disconnects between generations, the divisions we are dealing with today affect us all.

Unfortunately, these deep differences, which I call Generational Rifts, affect us in terms of goal-setting, achievement, and performance in both our personal and professional lives. Perhaps you will see yourself in these pages, or perhaps you will see people you interact with every day. The way that many of us view the world today—and whether we hear the branch creak—sometimes simply depends on how old we are.

Lots of books and articles have been written about the baby boomers, Generation X, the millennial generation, and Generation Z, and I will not regurgitate that information. Rather, I want to discuss these generations in relation to their hearing the branch creak and how to motivate them (and ourselves) to take action in the realms of education and workforce development. These thoughts are based on my in-depth work and actual experiences with schools and business advisory groups around the country. I have been successful in helping schools and associations nationwide enroll and retain more of the right students, in the right programs, for the right reasons, thereby elevating their performance. The principle is the same for employers who have benefited from my insights to recruit and retain more of the right workers, in the right positions, for the right reasons. To accomplish this goal we need to understand all the generations, but especially the Why Generation—comprising the groups commonly labeled as Generations Y and Z.

From here on, I will refer to both the millennials and Generation Z as simply the Why Generation. This name illustrates a core trait: in every context, these generations want to know why something is important. Why should they do it this way or that way? Why is a particular step important in the grand scheme of things? Their desire to understand the reason and purpose behind everything almost seems inborn, because this is how they've been taught to think and interact with the world. The "why" trait that defines these generations exists because we reared them this way. And yet, when I say this in front of business and industry groups, they often have an "aha" moment—the idea simply has not occurred to them.

Have you ever heard or experienced an exchange with a teacher, mentor, trainer, or superior that went something like this?

Trainee: "Why should I do it this way?"

Trainer: "Because I said so."

This conversation will get you nowhere with a member of the Why Generation. If you're part of the younger generations, you probably just cringed. This type of exchange would turn you off and crush your spirit. Young people truly want and need to understand why things are done a certain way because it lends credibility to their participation. If they see no logical reason for the effort, they will not put in a great deal of energy. They want their contribution to mean something. In fact, they want to determine for themselves if there is a better way to do it and if there is something they can add to make it better for everyone. It's not about challenging authority, but improving the process and outcome as a team player.

If we want to better understand how to unlock the potential of young people in a way that allows them to build fulfilling and productive lives, we need to meet them where they are rather than complain about why they aren't like us. We must grasp what makes them tick and why they do the things they do. It may come as a surprise, but they often have excellent reasons for their ideas, based on their different experience and perception of the world.

As with any generational discussion, there are outliers, people who fall outside the bell curve of their generation's norms. For purposes of our exploration, we will focus on the middle of the bell curve and discuss the characteristics of the overwhelming majority of the younger generations.

Let's start with a quick recap of the generations and their approximate ages today. I say approximate ages because there is fluidity between the end of one generation and the beginning of the next. Rarely does any one accepted date range define a generation. So if you permit me the latitude to use these dates, I have listed several generations with the years they were born, along with their most common nicknames.

Most Common Name	Birth Years
Lost Generation	1883–1900
Greatest Generation	1901–1924
Silent Generation	1925–1945
Baby Boom Generation	1946–1964
Generation X (MTV)	1965–1978
Why Generation (Millennial and Z-Generations)	1979–20??

These dates allow you to easily determine the generation to which you belong. For the Why Generation, you'll see that I haven't put an end date on the growth since they will also represent the generations to come. Throughout this book I will focus on three generational cohorts, which are the greatest generation, the baby boom generation, and the Why Generation.

I am passing over Generation X because in many instances, if you are in the younger half of Generation X, your traits tend to identify more closely with the Why Generation, and if you are in the older half of Generation X, your traits tend to identify more closely with the baby boom generation. Many of the traits we will cover for the Why Generation apply to roughly anyone under the age of 40.

These are our sons and daughters, coworkers, students, employees, and a significant number of the people we come into contact with daily. Maybe you're part of this age group yourself. Let's take a look at what distinguishes each generation from the others and the strengths and challenges of each.

Generational Profiles

The greatest generation earned its nickname because of Tom Brokaw's book titled simply that, *The Greatest Generation*. He called them that because of their great service to their country. They grew up in the Great Depression and in young adulthood fought in World War II. It is important to note that fighting in World War II did not just mean male GIs serving in the armed forces. It also meant women in tremendous numbers working to aid the war effort by building airplanes, submarines, tanks, and the critical infrastructure needed to move this country forward. This entire generation unselfishly gave of themselves to turn the tide during a critical moment in this country and the world.

We were fighting on two fronts against two enemies determined to crush us in their quest for total world domination. Our country was stretched thin and we had limited resources for both campaigns. This generation stepped up to the challenge not for appreciation, celebrity, or a big fat paycheck—but simply because it was the right thing to do. On a global scale, this generation heard the branch creak and knew something significant had to be done. They took responsibility and secured our freedom with their sacrifice, and upon returning from the war they built the United States into a global superpower.

The greatest generation is largely responsible for giving birth to the baby boom generation in the years following the war. The baby boom generation is the largest generation in American history, with over 76 million people born during those years. It is a huge bubble on the timeline of life and one we hear about constantly. The boomers are doing this and the boomers are doing that. Now the boomers are starting to retire, and we hear about how that will affect everything from our financial markets to the workforce. By far, they are the most financially successful generation in American history. They have created tremendous wealth, security, and opportunity.

The baby boom generation is largely responsible for giving birth to the Why Generation who, as a whole, total more than 100 million young people. To understand the massive size of both generations it is important to note that Generation X, sandwiched between these generations, is made up of approximately 43 million Americans.

This brings us to the Why Generation and how this cohort differs from those that came before. Unfortunately, the popular view of the younger generations today is not always a positive one. Young people don't understand respect, they don't have a good work ethic, they don't care about their futures, they're entitled, they're lazy, they're unengaged—I could go on and on. While there are certainly individuals within the younger generations that fit this profile, this is not the picture I see every day working with schools and businesses around the country. I see young people achieving truly exceptional things—meeting the high expectations placed upon them by their parents, teachers, and employers.

Because of the dominant negative stereotypes out there, many books and articles advise us to adjust (read: lower) our expectations for young people. Change the rules so everybody can win; make it easy to put in minimal effort to reach the next grade or goal or graduation. We must expect less; the old standards don't matter anymore. The assumption is that our young people just don't have it in them to perform at a higher level, so to avoid conflict, frustration, and disappointment, the best way of dealing with them is to bring things down to their perceived level.

What a mistake.

Our expectations are the first measure by which our young people judge their own capabilities. In effect, we tell them what's possible through our assumptions. Lowering our expectations and standards will not inspire them to achieve anything beyond that status quo. Making it too easy to reach the next goal renders that next goal meaningless.

We need to think differently about the younger generations. Far from expecting less, we can set the bar higher for their performance. I believe that today's young people do want to find that spark and make their mark on the world; many simply lack the guidance that will best motivate and inspire them in that direction. They need to find their passion. By using strategies that speak to the younger generations, like the **Light at the End of the Tunnel** and others we will discuss further, we can help them discover their dreams.

The Why Generation has grown up in a time of unprecedented technological advances that have changed every aspect of life and communication. Amid these challenges (and opportunities) that are unique in the history of the world, these young people are tenacious and talented. They have immense resources and abilities to change the world for the better, and not only that, but they want to. They value collaboration and community. When they find a cause they believe in, they give it everything they've got. Yes, they're different from older people, but that's not necessarily bad. In fact, many times those differences are strengths, not weaknesses.

Maybe your students, children, and employees aren't performing at their peak potential today. In his well-known book *The 7 Habits of Highly Effective People*, Stephen R. Covey writes, "Treat a man as he is and he will remain as he is. Treat a man as he can and should be and he will become as he can and should be."[1] I would encourage you not to lower your expectations to accommodate their current performance. You have more influence with them than you think. Don't settle, and don't let them settle. Kick it up a notch and challenge them to do more, to be more. Believe that they can. And remember, they will meet the expectations we place on them—low or high.

Profound changes in our society and world have produced generations with radically different worldviews, expectations, and goals. To the frustration and dismay of older generations, I often point out that the young people of the Why Generation are exactly the way we made them. And this is actually a source of great hope because it makes sense and fits a model that we can understand and use to help them unlock their true potential. We will review this and much more, because to motivate the younger generations, we must understand what makes them tick and how to help them create a strong sense of urgency and healthy fear of loss in their everyday lives.

I see the Why Generation filled with some of the most remarkable and unique people yet born. There are so many young people who have untapped promise and possibilities. Contrary to popular opinion, I believe that they have it within themselves to be the next greatest generation because they are extremely intelligent, resourceful, and imaginative, and they have an uncanny ability to attain impressive levels of laser focus. They generously support the causes they believe in, despite the record college debt burden they bear.[2] When they see what they want, they move at warp speed to accomplish it.

That's where the Light at the End of the Tunnel (explored further in chapter five) becomes critical in showing them what's possible and the clear rewards of taking action—traveling through the tunnel to reach the reward. The only thing missing for this generation to step into the breach and become the next greatest generation is a national catalyst or branch creak, like World War II's challenge to our freedom. If such an event takes place in our modern world, we will see our young people rally their talents and abilities to overcome a national crisis by focusing, strategically planning, and taking action—massive action.

Generational Disconnect: A Tale of Two Perspectives

The biggest difference I see between older and younger generations is their view of whether they "live to work" or "work to live." The younger generations' clear mantra is "work to live." They do not view their job as the end-all but rather as a means to an end, and that end is the experiences and lifestyle they long for in their everyday life. At the same time, young people don't draw hard lines between work life and personal life, and that's one reason flexibility in their work schedules is so important to them. It's no longer about a work-life balance, but a work-life blend. Experience is everything, flexibility is paramount, and lifestyle is the most important consideration in any career decision or direction.

I recall reading a story several years ago about a 24-year-old female from the Why Generation working typical 9:00 a.m. to 5:00 p.m. office hours, Monday through Friday, making $45,000 per year. Most people might agree that $45,000 annually for a 24-year-old is a good income and that she should be proud of that significant accomplishment. However, this job prevented her from attending a yoga class offered in her hometown at 4:00 p.m. every Monday, Wednesday, and Friday. It wasn't offered in the evening or on weekends. If you are a Why Generation member and you want to take that yoga class, what do you do? If you guessed "quit your job," you're right! She quit her job, moved in with her parents, and took a job with flex hours that paid $25,000 per year. So what did that yoga class cost? That's right, a little over $20,000 per year.

Whenever I share this story with audiences, I start looking for reactions as I walk through the decisions she made to move back in with her parents and take a job working flex hours for so much less than she was making before—all so she could simply experience that yoga class. Some of the older members of the audience, baby boomers in their 50s and 60s, look astonished that someone would take an earnings and career step back to that degree to simply participate in a yoga class. Perhaps they are thinking, "That's crazy, why would you do that?" Maybe you feel the same way.

On the other side of the spectrum, I see many in the younger portion of the audience looking thrilled that one of their peers may have gotten it right. Perhaps they are thinking, "Good for her, she is doing exactly what she wants and she is experiencing the benefits of the yoga class she longed to take part in." That represents an amazing divergence in point of view within the same audience.

To understand it, you have to appreciate both perspectives. On the one hand you have the older generations that are more likely to espouse the "live to work" creed where working hard, getting ahead, and building on your accomplishments to climb the ladder of success is critical to happiness and stability.

But look at it a different way—the younger way. The Why Generation audience defines success as the attainment of meaningful lifestyle experiences and the freedom to live life to the fullest. It all depends on how you view it, and many young people view a negative reaction to the young woman's actions as a misinterpretation of what's important. Sure, she moved back in with her parents, but she wouldn't have done that unless she wanted to reconnect with them and build that relationship. Sure, she took a $20,000 annual pay cut to work flex hours, but moving back home lowered her living expenses. Let's not forget, she gets to take the yoga class three times a week, and that leaves Tuesday and Thursday open to take an additional class, give back to her community, take up a hobby, and perhaps even expand her social engagements and opportunities for more robust experiences.

In the younger person's perspective, she may have more spending money by living at home than she enjoyed in her previous position, where she likely had higher taxes and living expenses. And bear in mind, she has expanded her lifestyle experiences and personal quality of life, which was the objective all along—game, set, and match.

At the end of the day, older-generation spectators often leave this story thinking she's crazy, and younger generations tend to leave thinking she's a genius. That is the profound difference between the older and younger generations today. In the end, neither point of view is right or wrong, just distinctly based on where the audience members are sitting in their lives and what priorities they champion.

Adjusting how we view these vast generational differences allows us to adapt to the changing needs of our children, students, and employees. We must get over our assumptions of "this is how it's done" because those in our circle of influence may have a very different perspective. And different doesn't mean wrong. The sweet spot for helping young people make the climb in their career and perform at a higher level is assisting them in finding the perfect intersection of experience, adventure, and work. When they find meaningful experiences, adventure, and a mission in the work they do, then it transcends "work" and becomes a fun, motivational, and worthwhile pursuit. And once you begin to understand—and appreciate—who the Why Generation members are, you're that much closer to unlocking their potential.

CHAPTER TWO INSIGHTS

- Today, anyone in the Why Generation (under the age of 40) has the potential to accomplish amazing things.

- Generational Rifts are the significantly different perspectives held by various generational cohorts, such as the baby boomers and millennials, that can lead to frustration, misunderstanding, conflict, and ultimately lower performance in the classroom and workplace.

- We should resist the tendency to lower our standards for the younger generations because they are fully capable of performing at a higher level and will respond to the expectations we create—positive or negative.

- While today's young people fall into many categories, we call them the Why Generation based largely on their need to understand the rationale for why they should do something and what's in it for them.

- The profoundly different views and values of the Why Generation members put them in conflict with older generations who often want them to conform to their own rules and priorities. This is a mistake. Our true opportunity is to unlock the potential of young people by meeting them in the middle.

- Different perspectives based on varying priorities between generations are not necessarily wrong—just different. When we can get past our assumption that the way we've always viewed things is the only or best way, we're that much closer to helping our young people maximize their performance.

CHAPTER THREE

Getting to Know the Why Generation

If I were to describe the younger generations in one key phrase, it would have to be that "experience is everything." They are hungry to experience life to the fullest and are looking for significant moments online, in person, on location, and through each relationship. "We'd rather have experiences than bank statements" is how one Why Generation member describes her generation's priorities.[1]

They learned this value from the original experience-is-everything generation of which I am a member, the baby boomers, but we didn't have the access that is available today. We had to find things to do, use our imagination, and invent ways to have fun. I recall throwing a tennis ball against the house for hours to keep myself occupied on low-action days. A Slinky® and an Etch A Sketch® could keep me amused indefinitely. My brothers and I spent a great amount of time outside with our friends exploring the world and all it had to offer. It's a different picture today.

Our circle of friends was important to us, but today's younger generations have raised friends to family status. They haven't lowered the importance of family—they have simply raised friends to the same status as family. Social media has become the blockbuster it is today because the younger generations want to communicate with and stay informed about their friends in ways we could not fathom years ago. We had a home phone, the ability to send and receive mail, and a bike to hop on to ride over to our friend's house—that was it. Today, you can update all your friends and followers instantly on Facebook, Instagram, Twitter, Pinterest, Snapchat, or any of the other seemingly infinite applications to communicate what you are doing, with whom you are doing it, and ultimately where you are investing your time and why. In addition, you can text, call, video chat, and conference call multiple friends in real time. Yes, a lot has changed.

This proliferation of material posted online has become staggering. After briefly meeting you, anyone can find your likes, dislikes, desires, and past successes and failures. In the baby boomers' younger years, we were more private and in some ways more secretive. Today people are an open book, transparently sharing their hopes, dreams, struggles, and thoughts with their social circle. Operating side by side with that "open book" philosophy is a naiveté about the permanency of content that is shared online. Contrary to popular opinion, the Internet is written in ink and in many instances cannot be erased. Content posted today is stored and cached on servers that are backed up indefinitely, which means the posts and pictures are forever "out there."

Such open sharing online can have big ramifications for future employment. Increasingly, employers are using the Internet to research and track potential hires and current employees to judge their habits and discern the right fit for certain positions and respon-sibilities. I know of a recent situation where a finalist for a senior-level VP position in a large organization was at the final hurdle prior to being chosen for the role. It was down to two worthy candidates. The organization went online, researched both candidates' online profiles, and found in one an alternative lifestyle. The alternative lifestyle itself was not an issue, but some of the links in the profile were potentially disturbing. With all else being equal, the other can-didate received the offer. What we post online makes a difference.

Today, the younger generations embody this experience-is-everything concept. They hunger, work, and seemingly exist for new and exhilarating experiences. They want to give back—many of the younger members of the Why Generation get excited about the potential to engage in vigorous involvement and volunteerism for the causes they believe in. They are socially conscious and envi-ronmentally responsible, and they have a great desire to explore and experience the world. These are highly positive traits that give us an extraordinary advantage in connecting with them, because if their "want-to" is strong enough, their "how-to" will come. This is a key motivational truth that we'll look at in more depth later, but for now, the "want-to" creates the strong sense of urgency while the goal they want to achieve keeps them focused and helps them find "how-to" achieve higher levels of performance. Their desire for experiences can be the greatest self-motivating tool available to help move them for-ward. The more you understand their need for experiences and which experiences are most important to them, the more you will be able to communicate as a trusted ally in gaining those desired experiences.

Unique, Special, and Important

I thought growing up that we were all individuals striving to fit in with a world that was rapidly and sometimes violently changing. We all developed a keen sense of individuality, but the young people of the Why Generation have taken their individual nature to a whole new level. Three words that best describe and encapsulate them are *unique, special,* and *important.*

The words *unique, special,* and *important* seem to flow together as one, so I will use them that way. As a result of being reared in a remarkably nurtured and supported manner, today's young people have developed a strong sense of unique individuality, a feeling that they are special, and a strong conviction that they are important. Is this you? It's a great thing to believe in yourself! I want to cover it in depth because it's a belief that has deep ramifications for educators, employers, and parents engaging today's young people. Because of this belief, the Why Generation is the most forthcoming, open, and privacy-averse generation yet. As we've discussed, many openly share their lives on the Internet and social media, in person, and whenever the opportunity arises to tell their story.

Their uniqueness is undeniable and can be seen everywhere. They have customized and personalized their entire lives, as shown in the way they use technology and communicate via social media. Why Generation members strive to be unique and set themselves apart from their peers. To this generation, being unique means embracing your distinctive nature and sharing it with the world, in many cases. Look at the way they personalize their cell phone wallpaper, set special ringtones for each friend, and configure their social network to post on the vast array of social media tools and sites available to share their experiences. This prioritization of uniqueness is a valuable asset because they will always work hard to stand out in a crowded field.

As a part of their uniqueness, this generation celebrates diversity. They have also developed an uncanny knack for rewriting the rules. Case in point: At 12 years old, my son Matt earned the nickname "Dr. Loophole" because he could always find a legal way around every rule I established in the house. "Well, you never said we couldn't do it this way, Dad," became an all-too-frequent comeback during disciplinary engagements.

Moreover, they have extremely high expectations of everything around them, including their family, friends, education system, employers, and community. In fact, they often have lofty expectations of everything in their lives, except, seemingly, for one thing—themselves. Despite having so many advantages, talents, and skills, they expect far less from themselves than they are truly capable of achieving.

Group Emphasis

The Why Generation generally prefers the group dynamic to one-on-one interaction. In fact, if you see young people today on a date, what you'll probably see is a group. It is what I lovingly refer to as "pack dating." The reason is simple: social interaction is easier and can be much more fun in a group setting.

As an example, if I were to go on a date, the social interaction would work in a seesaw kind of exchange. When I am done talking, it's her turn, and when she is done talking, it's my turn. Our society dictates that in a one-on-one interchange, it is the responsibility of one party to speak in response to the other party's expression of ideas or communication. This can be a challenging dynamic and create some pressure for two people on their own. In a group setting, however, the social interaction and pressure can be greatly reduced, as there are many participants and people adding to the communication pie, so to speak. In other words, if you are out on a date with two additional couples, a total of six people, you do not have to carry the complete burden of conversation. You can chime in when you have something to share that you feel adds value to the interaction. Moreover, the fun that can be generated by a group can be significantly higher than in a one-on-one dating environment.

After all, experience is everything, and anything that brings more fun experiences is a great night out.

Because young people prefer group interactions to one-on-one interactions, there are incredible opportunities for sharing ideas, sparking dialogue, and mentoring them in group settings. This can happen in the classroom, in the workplace, or anywhere. It's one of the reasons that the younger generations tend to work so well as part of a team dynamic. Group collaboration does not exclude the possibility or power of individual interactions, but this insight into their preference for groups can be helpful when seeking to maximize results with young people.

Digital Natives

This may be obvious, but the Why Generation embraces technology. If you want to know what's going on in the world of technology, simply ask a young person. He or she will, at the very least, point you in the right direction and in many cases give you the full scoop. As early adopters of all things tech, both of my sons Matt and Nick are proud nerds who wear that distinction like a badge of honor. If I want to know what's going on in the world, I simply talk with my sons. They always seem to know what the latest and greatest is for almost everything. I no longer hook up my own electronics; Matt does it all. He knows what I need, where to get it, and how to install it, and he gets it up and running in pit-crew speed. Sure, I could do it myself—but asking him is way easier. They also have their fingers on the pulse of everything related to darn near everything. I am amazed at the discussions we have about TV shows, movies, video games, pop culture, local and national news, and world events. They know what's going on, yet they never watch the news.

Today there are hundreds of TV channels and seemingly end-less choices. This technological boom, which has given us cable and satellite TV, on-demand programming, digital video recorders, streaming audio and video, high-speed broadband Internet, video conferencing, smartphones, texting, instant messaging, and social network integration has created an amazing number of choices—but also a tremendous number of distractions.

My sons don't simply watch TV. They turn on a program via TV, video on demand, Netflix, Hulu, or some comparable streaming service while they surf the Internet from their laptop and text or update social media using their smartphone or tablet. They are always multitasking and in search mode for the next fun or interesting experience. With all of these easy connections, many options, and an unlimited supply of distractions, it is easy for this generation to lose focus inside their ballet of multitasking.

Focus has become a finite, narrowly defined period of time for the Why Generation—and frankly, even for older generations. Young people no longer have time for a long, drawn-out experience—they hunger for numerous short, cool experiences. Even the messages we send have become short message fragments of 280 characters or less. Younger members of the Why Generation especially value instant communication and online repartee, often sacrificing clarity for speed.[2] The world has changed from the days when you wrote a letter to a friend or family member and took a long time to think it through, write it out, and revise it. Today, young people impulsively share their thoughts in the blink of an eye, posting them for the world to see—which can cause Generational Rifts with older people who often see this as one more indication of young people's annoying sense of self-focused entitlement.

The Entitlement Factor

Let's look at the implications of what this so-called "entitled mindset" of the Why Generation means to us. The expectations of today's younger generations are vastly different from those of their older coworkers. Due in large part to the coddling they received growing up, they expect a significant amount of attention from their employers. In some cases, they become high maintenance because an annual or even semiannual performance review is not nearly enough to meet their need for constant feedback, praise, and guidance so they can feel comfortable in their positions. In addition, a bad review can be devastating to some young workers, as they are not used to hearing negative feedback.

Their expectations in the workplace also differ from those of older workers who have accepted that advancement, bonuses, perks, and vacation time are all earned and take time to attain. According to a survey of hiring managers and human resource executives, more than 85 percent of those surveyed stated that members of the Why Generation have a stronger sense of entitlement than older workers.[3]

Purpose and vision aside, what Why Generation members want the most from their work is as follows:

- higher pay
- flexible work schedules
- promotion within one year
- more vacation or personal time

To punctuate that point, several years ago I was chatting over dinner with a longtime friend and client who was telling me about her son who had recently graduated from Ohio State University with a degree in finance. He had accepted a position at one of the large national banks headquartered in Charlotte, North Carolina, and had worked there nine months when he called to let her know that he had received a huge promotion and significant raise. Naturally, she was proud of her son, but what he said next floored her. After nine months on the job, he actually said, "I am thrilled because this was a long time coming." A long time coming? He had only worked there nine months, and yet the expectation was that praise, promotion, and more money were all a foregone conclusion.

As a young baby boomer and one of the younger members of my generation who experienced a vastly different childhood from my friend's Why Generation son, I had no such expectations for my first work experience coming out of college. I was hired as a sales representative by a national business forms printing manufacturer headquartered in Chicago with offices nationwide. It was the largest company of its kind in the United States, and I worked in their Cleveland office alongside lots of established and successful salespeople. I spent my entire first month sitting in the conference room training myself by reading several huge binders of coursework to gain an understanding of the printing industry. It was remarkably unfulfilling. At the end of the first year I was lucky I was still employed—and there were no expectations for much praise, promotion, and more money. The world has changed since I joined the workforce, and, based on everything I have learned since, we can no longer operate under the old assumptions that applied back then.

"Older people like me have to understand where younger people are coming from," says Cathie Raymond, deputy associate superintendent and state CTE director for the state of Arizona. "The times they are a-changing," she says. "Older people need to understand the different strengths and creativity that younger people bring to the table. At the same time, young people also need to understand that their expectations for what they want may be high. In the end, we all face the question of either working with young people or working against them."[4]

Employers who don't adapt to the traits of their younger workers will fail to retain those workers over the long term and will thus compromise their company's future success. It's not only about the salary anymore; today's young people demand a workplace that stimulates their creativity, values their contribution, and challenges them to exceed their limits as they work toward a shared vision they believe in. Far from being lazy and apathetic, the younger generations truly want to achieve great things in their careers—but on their terms. And those terms include a company direction that aligns with their core beliefs and makes the world a better place in some way. As one member of the Why Generation puts it, "We're not going to hand our souls over to men in suits or women in pencil skirts. We're not going to work for companies we don't respect. We're not going to wake up every morning dreading the 9-to-5. But we're not going to sit back and sulk either . . . We don't pursue the paycheck, we pursue the passion."[5] If you're an employer, are you hearing a branch creak here?

When we understand the traits of the younger generations, we can make the most of our interactions with them. These insights and suggestions are valuable not just for employers interacting with younger workers, but also for parents relating to their children, educators working with their students, and anyone who engages with the younger generations on a daily basis. And if you're part of the younger generations, perhaps these observations will help you understand your own strengths and struggles in all these contexts.

As we discussed earlier, the younger generations prefer group interactions to one-on-one interactions, so they work well in team-oriented situations. They thrive in a brainstorming and idea-sharing environment where they can contribute to the direction and outcomes of the group. This gives them an excellent opportunity to place their unique, special, and important seal on the team and the success of the project. They take great pride in being part of a winning team and contributing their individuality to that team.

What's more, these generations will work hard for what they

want—especially younger members of the Why Generation. They're going to work earlier (often encouraged to do so by their parents), looking to gain experience and start creating the economic security they're seeking. This comes from their concern about the future. They've been growing up in a post-9/11 world of uncertainty, and many have witnessed the struggles of parents and older siblings following the economic downturn of 2008. As a result, younger members of the Why Generation differ slightly from their older counterparts in that they have a stronger motivation to achieve economic security.

They are also good multitaskers. Look at any young person's computer screen and you will see many open web browser tabs, multiple programs and projects in various stages of completion, music playing, videos streaming—and yet with all these distractions they are still capable of completing their assigned tasks. And that's just the computer; there are also their phones, TVs, tablets, and other devices. It's a different way to work, but not necessarily a bad one in today's media-driven world. Personally, I'm always amazed at what young people are able to achieve in the sea of distractions and advertisements screaming for their attention. The key takeaway here is that they do not become overwhelmed with many simultaneous tasks, but rather thrive on the stimulation that multitasking affords.

Because they are in a constant search for experiences—experience is everything—they insist on a stimulating environment. Whether at home, in school, or at work, they thrive in an appealing, fun, and dynamic setting that creates the opportunity for many interesting experiences.

Employers often struggle to explain why they ask their employees to do something in a specific way because the Why Generation doesn't accept an answer of "because that's how we've always done it." If you want to activate young people, you need to connect them with the reasoning behind your decisions. They are the

Why Generation, after all. United Parcel Service (UPS) is one such employer that has embraced this change.[6] They have been investing heavily in overcoming challenges with their younger-generation workers since mid-2000, when they realized that their retention rates were dropping among younger workers in this generation. Even though UPS drivers earn an average of $95,000 per year including benefits, the retention loss rate for younger drivers was staggering. Despite the money, ultimately these employees were overwhelmed by the company's "340 methods" (actually many more than that now) that were taught to them via lecture format during a two-week training period. This training format simply wasn't enough for these young people to grasp the unexpected intricacies and demands of the job. The company realized that their training process for new drivers was out of date and out of touch with the learning habits of their younger audience.

After spending millions of dollars, UPS created a cool, high-tech training facility and curriculum to try to improve their retention rates among the younger generations. As one of the most structured companies in the United States, they have broken every part of the job down to a strategic process—including how to enter and leave what the company calls its "package cars." Getting off the truck is a five-step method, while getting on it involves three steps. This new training incorporates an instruction manual that includes how you grab a package, how you use the handrails when climbing or descending steps, how you bend your knees, and how you hold the position of your back. Overkill, you say? Well, the new training classes take place in a simulated truck made of see-through material and filled with sensors—on the floor, in the handrails, and on the steps—that record a trainee's movements and allow the trainers to capture a ton of data. Working at UPS is physical work where you are constantly moving and carrying heavy packages throughout the day. Every movement you make can take its toll on your body. The trainers don't just tell but *show* young trainees what the impact is on their bodies from entering and exiting the truck both their way and the prescribed way. They're even able to compute and quantify the physical wear and tear of a trainee's unpracticed method of getting on and off the truck to state how many years that person can work injury free. Using the UPS method, it could be the entirety of the career; using the trainee's unpracticed method, it could be only a few years before injury takes place. Said another way, they explain *why* they ask drivers to do things a certain way. The result has been that UPS has created a way to better engage and retain its most promising Why Generation employees.

Do We Really Have to Kiss Their Butts?

As I interact with CEOs and hiring managers, I have discovered a huge misunderstanding in their view of the younger generations. These major employers believe that to get their younger employees to be productive and stay at their company, they have to kiss their butts. I have actually heard them say, "We do not want to kiss their ass just to get a day's work out of them." Butt-kissing: that's what these employers have taken from all the generational information and advice that's out there. No wonder we are dealing with such a massive generational divide in this country! Given the largely negative and false stereotypes circulating about these generations, I can understand how someone might arrive at this conclusion. But nothing could be further from reality.

Yes, experience is everything, but vision and mission are the most important elements of the experience. Young people want to believe in something bigger than themselves. They want to make money to fund their lifestyle, sure, but they also want to give back and be a part of something unique, special, and important—like themselves. The butt-kissing approach misses this point completely.

It looks different from company to company, but often takes the form of simply giving the younger employees stuff. And mere stuff is not what these workers are looking for. As Niraj Chokshi wrote on *The Washington Post* blog: "Working [young people] ask a lot of their employers, but game rooms and rock walls are low on the list."[7] A 2015 survey by Accenture found that 59 percent of recent graduates said they would rather work in a company with a positive social atmosphere than a place with a higher salary, and 52 percent said they would forego some compensation to work at a company with a strong commitment to the environment or the social impact of its products and services.[8] Members of the Why Generation need to see what I call a Light at the End of the Tunnel, and their light must connect to something worthwhile, meaningful, and dare I say, cool.

An example of a company that has tried to create the kind of workplace young people would find attractive is Kimberly-Clark.[9] They offer a range of programs that include on-the-job training, continuing education, and workshops as a way to recruit and retain young employees. The company encourages its employees to strike a healthy work-life balance by offering flexible work schedules and the ability to work from home. They also offer employees access to loaner bicycles and shower facilities at work to encourage people to bike to work.

Perhaps equally important, Kimberly-Clark understands how today's young people want their ideas to be heard—and acted on when possible. The company launched what it calls its Welcome Original Thinkers program, which is designed to attract the best and brightest employees motivated to work somewhere where they can make a difference from day one in a company that operates in a socially responsible way.

But not every company has been able or willing to make this shift. One of the companies I've spoken to about this issue pushed back on the idea of making its workplace distinctive and fun because its leadership felt their particular business didn't have a plausible opportunity to do so. I suggested creating ways that internal departments could compete to give back in the community, such as Habitat for Humanity, St. Jude Children's Research Hospital, the local food bank, and others. I told them to find ways to get employees involved and match contributions and efforts to some extent, because this would create teams of people (a favorite social dynamic of the younger generations) who were pulling in the same direction (achieving a united sense of purpose and mission). This company's biggest challenge was that it didn't have the ability to compete on the field of fun and unusual office-lifestyle enhancements. But it could compete on the larger stage by creating a worthwhile vision and mission for each department to give back to the community. This type of outward focus gives the younger workers something to connect to and positions the organization as the connective tissue in being part of something bigger and making a difference.

Many times it seems that companies would prefer to continue doing things the way they have always done them, or make only token steps toward a more vision-centric company ethic. It's as if the older and younger generations are on different ends of a spectrum, and employers feel they have to move toward the younger generations—but they would prefer that the younger people would instead move in the direction of the employer. We have to let go of that expectation and work toward mutual success, viewing younger employees not as problems to be managed but as assets to be developed and valued. We don't appease or kiss up to them; we partner with them in a meaningful mission that brings purpose and value beyond just the paycheck. Quite simply, a successful 21st-century recruitment and retention strategy is not about kowtowing to the younger employees' desires. It's about harnessing their need for purpose, lighting up their pathway, and offering them something powerful to believe in. It's not about giving them stuff; it's entirely about inspiring them. It's how I run my business at TFS—and it works.

Where's the Loyalty?

Many things have changed in the workforce of today, and one of the bigger shifts is in the area of loyalty. It is not nearly what it was decades ago—and that shift goes both ways. There was a time when people worked for a company and stayed at that company for a long time, perhaps even their entire career. They moved up, earned more, established a positive work history, and retired with a rewarding pension and retirement plan. They were loyal to the company, and the company was loyal to them.

Things have changed on both sides. Young employees are no longer as loyal to a company because they are more loyal to several ideals already discussed: they want a stimulating work and education environment where they are free to use their individuality, creativity, and efforts to put their unique, special, and important seal on their team's and company's success. If that does not seem possible, they will likely search for a company and position where that can happen. Likewise, employers are no longer as loyal to their employees due to the pressures, business needs, and rapid pace of staying on the edge of global commerce. The loss of loyalty is a two-way street and has become the new reality in the American labor market.

When I was starting out in my career, the advice was not to litter your résumé with lots of jobs because that would indicate to an employer that you were not loyal and could potentially jump ship at any time. This philosophy has drastically changed or at least been supplanted by the notion that the more things you try, the better the chance that you will find the right fit and experience. This could be evidenced by reviewing the résumé of a typical 20-something pre-2008. Even at such a young age, it was likely a multipage document with change occurring about every 18 to 24 months. The 2008 meltdown, when jobs became scarce, created a challenging time for members of the Why Generation who were of working age, as they were either pigeonholed where they were or lost their job altogether without the prospect of finding a new one any time soon.

As I've said, loyalty is not lacking only among younger employees. Due to competing on a global stage, many companies are not nearly as loyal to their employees today as they were in the past. Downsizing, rightsizing, offshoring, outsourcing, and layoffs have become the norm during challenging economic times. Companies are struggling to compete, and the new normal is doing more with significantly less.

Not only that, but many in the younger generations are looking for opportunities to be their own boss. For those members of the Why Generation who are independent and innovative, the freedom and responsibility of entrepreneurship can be attractive. The independence of doing their own thing or being in full control can appear enticing enough to pluck the younger generations from the traditional workforce at a time when many employers are struggling to find and retain the best talent possible. The challenge for employers is to create that same valuable independence within their organizations that allows the younger generations to work within an existing structure but also feel they have the autonomy, authority, and self-directed work opportunities that deliver the best of both worlds. This can sow the seeds of loyalty and deep pride for a vision achieved on their own terms.

My Why Gen Team at TFS

I consider today's young people remarkable because of their instinctive desire to solve challenges and find a better way. There's a good reason that my team at TFS is largely made up of members of the

Why Generation: each and every one of them is focused, hard-working, and passionate about accomplishing great things within our organization. They see the vision, the Light at the End of the Tunnel, and have a profound desire to be a part of an organization that is making a difference. This is at the heart of their performance, and it drives them to amazing heights. "My Why Gen-ers," as I call them, work all hours of the day, night, weekends, and holidays as needed—not because I make them, but because they are vested, excited, and frankly all-in on achieving something great. They have many of the same traits described in these pages, and yet they excel beyond many others in their generation. So why is that? Perhaps it's because they see a clear vision, are treated well, and feel respected for their significant contribution to the difference we are making.

I have no greater thrill than when I sit in our conference room, pull the pin on the grenade of ideas, and toss it into the center of the room. I am confident and proud that my Why Generation folks will solve any challenge that arises within our organization and business model. The secret: I lead them with a clear vision and allow them the flexibility, responsibility, and accountability to make decisions for the betterment of our clients and company. I empower them and hold them accountable for the outcome that they share as an equal partner in making a difference for our clients in education and workforce development across North America. When they ask why, I always respond with a detailed answer and leave plenty of room for their perspective. They have a unique ability to see past where I or others were able to take the process and envision fresh enhancements, ideas, and innovations. Hear me, younger generations: you have incredible contributions to make, whether you realize it or not!

CHAPTER THREE INSIGHTS

- You can summarize the attitude of the Why Generation in a single expression: experience is everything. Young people today are much more likely to prioritize their lifestyle choices over anything else.

- The young people of the Why Generation have been raised to believe they are unique, special, and important. They are also quick to embrace diversity and to question any rules imposed on them.

- Why Generation members generally prefer to operate in packs in everything they do—both at work and with their friends.

- It goes without question that today's young people have been born with technology in their hands. Technology is a part of their daily lives. It's how they expect to work, play, and connect with each other.

- Many young people have been labeled as being entitled—which can often lead them into conflict with older generations. Young people are also much more likely to job-hop in pursuit of work that awards them the lifestyle they want. This is an important insight for employers looking for ways to both recruit and retain top young talent.

- Taking the time to tell and show Why Generation members the reasons for the things they're expected to do will engage them at a deeper level and validate their need to know, as UPS's transformation of their training program illustrates. Kimberly-Clark is another global company that is being intentional about keeping pace with the priorities of their younger workforce.

- We don't have to pander to the younger generations to get them to perform; instead, they will deliver incredible results when we answer their "why?" with a compelling vision and mission for what we're asking them to do.

- Loyalty has changed on both sides in the workplace, and many young people, especially Generation Z, have a strong entrepreneurial bent.

- Today's young people have incredible potential that I see in action every day with my Why Gen team.

Plan for Exceptional Performance

CHAPTER FOUR

Why the Why Generation Doesn't Hear the Branch Creaking

Today's younger generations, more than any previous generation, seldom if ever hear the branch creak underneath their feet. (A notable exception would be the younger members of the Why Generation who grew up witnessing the effects of the 2008 economic downturn on their parents' and older siblings' careers and are thus more concerned about their own economic prospects.) When I have asked audiences why most of today's young people do not hear the branch creak, participants have contributed such suggestions as "they're too comfortable"; "they take few chances"; "they rarely climb the tree"; and "they hardly ever go outside." All accurate answers—and yet the most enlightening reason is that they are for the most part the sons and daughters of the most financially successful generations in history, the baby boomers and Generation

X, and no matter where they sit today—upper, middle, or lower income—their situation is not that bad. They can always move back home with their parents, crash at a buddy's house, or find a place to lay their head at night. Even at the lower-income end of the spectrum, there are state and local support services available to lend a helping hand. "Our chickens are coming home to roost," says David Sload, the president and CEO of the Associated Builders and Contractors Keystone Chapter in Pennsylvania. "I think there is a dawning realization that as the number of people living with their parents without a job increases, we are entering a crisis. The fact is that college is not for everyone, especially at 18 years old. That narrative that you need to go to college has done us all a disservice that's led us to our current under-employment problem."[1]

I think we can all agree that we might need a more sustainable model.

And to do that, we first need to acknowledge that the Why Generation has been raised for achievement. They have been generously praised both when they have done well and sometimes when they have done poorly, to avoid damaging their self-esteem. Their parents (and therefore, they) have placed a huge importance on racking up accomplishments both inside and outside the classroom. Parents, teachers, coaches, and friends have affirmed them throughout their childhood with seemingly endless strings of praise and positive comments. These ongoing accolades have become critical to their self-esteem and have led to a desire for a great deal of continuing attention.

They have been nicknamed the "trophy kids," because in many parts of this country trophies are provided for everyone who participates in a sport. Not just the winning team, but everyone who plays receives a trophy. You have to ask, if everyone receives a trophy, does the trophy mean anything—to anyone? In this circumstance, it appears we have watered down achievement to the lowest common denominator in an effort to avoid hurting anyone's feelings while artificially boosting self-esteem. But if self-esteem comes from within and represents what we think of ourselves, is it possible to artificially create it?

Entitlement also grows out of a sense of being right—even when you are wrong. Through our efforts to bolster their self-esteem, these generations have grown up rarely being told they are wrong. The deck has been stacked in some cases to ensure they do not hear the branch creak or feel the shame of being wrong. But growth happens when you are wrong, the branch creaks, and you face the consequences of your actions. If consequences don't occur, a feeling of always being right (and therefore entitled) can result. This can be seen in schools across the country as far too many students are doing less work but still expecting to graduate all the same and simply move on.

As an example, it has become easier and easier for a student to catch up on deficient credits in high school, especially at the last minute, because schools are under fire to graduate their students and move them on into some kind of positive placement such as college, career training, the military, and so on. A credit-deficient student does not have enough credits to graduate because somewhere along the line he or she has not taken or passed enough of the right courses. Sometimes this situation arises because of the courses these students took, the performance they delivered, or just plain laziness and lack of engagement. For whatever reason, these students become at risk of not graduating. In our society and school systems today, this is considered a failure not only of the student, but also the school, the community, the state, and the education system in general. Everyone loses—so what's the answer when everyone loses? We must make sure they get the credits and move on, because that is in everyone's best interest according to the way our education system is evaluated and funded.

I know counselors, teachers, and administrators who hound students to make up their credits by staying after school, coming in early, or working harder. As reported to me, many credit-deficient students exhibit a total lack of interest in doing the necessary work because they know that at the last minute and in the final hours there will be an easy fix to their situation. I have been told by counselors that some students will say, "Why should I try during the school year when I can get an easy credit online from home in a few weeks?" The students are smart; they've come to understand the way the system works, and consequently many have figured out the bare minimum necessary to simply get through. There appears to be no branch creak, little consequence, and certainly no Light at the End of the Tunnel for these students. If there is no urgency, no "want-to," then there is no "how-to" leading to performance. Consider the long-term effects of this system on students today who become the employees of tomorrow. Have we taught them to strive with all their might for what they want—or to do as little as possible to get by?

In my travels, I speak to many diverse education groups, and I always ask teachers in the audience, "Have you ever looked into the eyes of a student and clearly wanted it more for them than they wanted it for themselves?" Teachers nod in complete agreement and some articulate out loud that it happens every day. In a dream-state kind of way, many of them feel like they would love to hold the student up against the wall by the collar in an effort to get through and state directly, "Do you realize the options and opportunities that are passing you by every day? Do you have any idea of the amazing possibilities within your reach? Wake up!"

I submit to you that these students simply don't hear the branch creak. They are pretty comfortable, and growth is a far-off, "maturity" kind of concept that happens when they are much older, certainly not today. But growth happens when we step outside our comfort zone, when the branch creaks—almost never when we are in our comfort zone standing on firm ground.

We should think about the safety nets we've created for our children and students—and maybe also ourselves. Should those safety nets be removed? Branch creaks mean nothing if there's no real danger of plunging to the ground below. Short-term discomfort can be the catalyst for long-term positive change—and that might start with the parents.

Parenting: A Broad Spectrum

In general, today's younger generations have been nurtured and cared for to an extent unlike any previous generation. I've touched on this before, but it's an important truth to grasp where many of their traits come from. They have been supported, encouraged, and given a great many opportunities that were unavailable to their ancestors. Perhaps you have experienced life as part of this nurtured generation. Nurturing is essential and important, but how far should it be taken? Is there a point at which it goes from a positive to a negative?

My previous home had a robin's nest outside the front door. It was nestled inside a tall standing bush right in front of one of the two columns at the front door. What made this nest fun to watch was that it was easily visible from behind, where you could see it from the front porch. It was wonderful. I was able to get close and peer in to see the young occupants after they had hatched. Mother and father bird were always gracious in allowing me to catch a bird's-eye view of the action. I never lingered, just grabbed a quick look and moved back inside so as not to spook them.

No doubt, mother and father bird were wonderful, nurturing parents. They kept watch, defended, fed, and took care of any other needs their young had. I watched as the baby birds grew and reached their young adult stage. For several days the young birds began to fly in and out of the nest—testing their wings, developing strength, and acquiring the early signs of self-reliance and independence. After several days of this ballet of coming and going from the nest, the nest was empty. The entire family had moved on. Sure, the mother and father were still engaged in the lives of their young and would continue to feed them, but the goal of the process had been to wean them off parental support so they could fly, hunt, and care for themselves. This and many other examples of parenting exist in nature—parents helping their young develop the necessary skills to literally and figuratively fly on their own.

There are many kinds of parents: unengaged, engaged, and perhaps even overengaged. Are you familiar with the term *helicopter parents*? These are the parents who are constantly hovering over their sons and daughters, just as helicopters hover, to ensure that everything in their lives is going well and according to plan. As I said, the Why Generation has been nurtured unlike any previous generation. Due in part to technological advances that give us the ability to stay connected 24 hours a day, modern parents have unprecedented connection to their children.

I do not mean to suggest that helicopter parenting is completely negative, but it can flirt with the boundary between empowering and enabling. Are we ever allowing our children to fly on their own versus continually flapping their wings for them and feeding them? Could we be "helping" them beyond the time they can do it for themselves? And if we are, is that helping them achieve the results we truly want for them?

Through my work with schools across the country, I have heard shocking stories of helicopter parents interceding to make up for their son's or daughter's lack of performance in the classroom. It has even been reported that some helicopter parents wake up their adult children each morning at college or prior to the workday to ensure they are on time and on task. What's more, if something goes wrong, they are the first to be on the phone to correct the perceived injustice to their kids.

To be clear, I am 100 percent behind every parent's desire to be fully invested, fully behind, and fully supportive of their kids and their performance—parents, I am for you and with you. But there is a difference between covering for your child and supporting the learning process. As much as I wanted my sons to succeed in school, I have never been a fan of reversing a bad grade or making excuses to the teacher about a lack of performance displayed by either Matt or Nick. I believe in the idea that they should endure the consequences of their actions—all their actions. As a result, I always held them accountable to experience those consequences as part of the learning required to develop the long-term goal of self-reliance and independence.

When it comes to employment, are some parents going too far in supporting their children? You be the judge. A recent survey reported that a significant portion of business and industry hiring managers had received some kind of contact from the parents of the Why Generation candidates they were interviewing for a job. That's a pretty connected and engaged parent. At the same time, are we sure these fiercely supportive parents are supporting their kids' awareness of the vast opportunities before them—even if they don't go to college? I believe that what we are confronting is an Awareness Gap about the kinds of opportunities available to our children.

My parents loved me; there has never been a doubt of that. They would have done anything for my brothers and me and have been remarkably supportive throughout the course of my life. What they never did was make excuses for my lack of performance or help cover my butt when I was way out on the limb and the branch was about to creak because of my own decisions. The greatest lessons they taught me were during the times they left me to deal with

the consequences of my own actions alone—when I taught myself
because they allowed me to experience the penalties.

But it's also critical to acknowledge that some young people today
don't have helicopter or engaged parents. In fact, they might have
parents who have severely neglected or abused them—if their parents were in the picture at all. For these young people, their branch
creaked at far too young of an age. Many have either been kicked
out of their home or left on their own. Some students attend school
during the day and couch-surf at friends' houses at night. Others live
under a bridge. Some parents have been known to sneak their kids
into garages every night to sleep because they lack a suitable home.

Many parents struggle with their own lives while also trying to
rear their kids. They are real people dealing with real issues. I remember hearing a story about a six-year-old first-grader whose father left
for work by 7:00 a.m. every morning—leaving the child to feed
himself breakfast, lock the door, put the key under the mat, and
walk to the bus stop by himself. Mom was dealing with an addic-
tion and was not around. This six-year-old would then come home
to an empty house each day until his dad got home around dinner
time. Due to the relationship and mutual respect this student had
with his teacher, he eventually shared this secret reality with her. As
a result, he went to live with grandparents who were better able to
take care of him. And this is one of the milder cases; at least this
child had a home and a father. Many other children do not.

I share this story because every teacher knows stories like this
where the branch has creaked for their students at too young an
age. It helps explain why many students are insecure and lack self-
confidence, motivation, and the belief that they can achieve amazing things. There's also the threat of young people turning to drugs
as early as the sixth grade for many reasons that include curiosity,
bullying, and stress. Their branch has creaked in a different way and
they don't know how to deal with it. These young people have not

failed, but life circumstances over which they have no control have dealt them a challenging reality.

I believe part of the answer, in addition to teaching critical coping skills, is to show these young people that there is indeed a Light at the End of the Tunnel for them. They need to see that their hardships can potentially become advantages since they have learned not to just survive, but to thrive. Life may have knocked them down, but they got back up. One of the first things we have to do is build their hope that things can get better and they can rise above the challenges in their lives. We have to help them find their light and show them the way—their way—through the tunnel.

The statement "they don't care how much you know, until they know how much you care" is doubly true for students coming from disadvantaged backgrounds. They crave positive and happy people who take the time to share meaningful encouragement and support. Many have experienced not just a passive lack of affirmation, but its active opposite: put-downs and bullying. Although I believe a healthy self-esteem cannot be conferred and must come from within, some young people have become so used to negative messages that they need help framing positive affirmations that bring hope. When they feel respected, they reciprocate that respect quickly and work harder to achieve more. We have to believe they can do it because when we do, it's contagious, and they will start believing it too.

Whatever end of the parenting spectrum today's young people have experienced, I believe they have everything within themselves to be the next greatest generation. As I've said earlier, right now as a generation they simply lack the catalyst to ignite that fire. After all, the greatest generation of World War II didn't come out of the womb better than any other generation; they earned the nickname greatest generation as a result of the branch creaking for our country as we were thrust into a two-theater war in Europe and the Pacific that threatened our freedom.

The Why Generation has the intelligence, resources, and pit bull–like tenacity to step into the breach when called on by our country to make a difference in the face of a major national crisis. It will happen when and if the branch creaks and they feel the heavy weight of a country in danger. That healthy fear of loss and sense of urgency will ignite their spirit, require their knowledge, take advantage of their desire to give back, and demand their attention in a way they have not experienced before. It is at that time that we as a nation will be forced to focus on the challenges at hand, strategically plan a suitable course, and take massive action to neutralize the impending threats that come our way.

I consider this a powerful message of hope as it relates to the ability of the Why Generation to solve the next round of challenges our country faces. Together we can move forward in a world where the landscape is always shifting under our feet, and all too often the branch seems overloaded with the weight of so many out on the limb.

The Power of Failure

When I look back over the course of my life, I do not see a straight and well-defined path that would be easy to replicate. I see countless milestones, accomplishments—and every so often, failures—that added up to a lifetime of learning experiences where each time the branch creaked I focused, planned, and took action. Each of those seeming setbacks came at an initial cost to my self-esteem, but in hindsight they have made all the difference. Integrity and character are forged when we are up against it, fighting back, picking ourselves up after being knocked down, and overcoming what may feel like insurmountable odds to achieve beyond expectations. Those are the moments to be proud and relish the power of the human spirit.

I do not know a successful person who never failed. Yet failure seems to be avoided at all costs today in an effort to create positive self-esteem and ensure we simply keep young people advancing to the next step. Are we doing them a disservice? The latest research from cognitive science seems to indicate we might be—and that the most effective and memorable learning takes place after we make mistakes.[2] It seems we may be biologically wired in a way that we focus more after we err—especially if we were highly confident that we hadn't made a mistake. It's like thinking you aced a test and finding out you scored a low grade. After that experience, you are better motivated and able to focus on relearning the material. Failing really does make us stronger; it can bring out our best selves. This is exactly what happens when you hear the branch creak and become instantly primed to focus, plan, and take action.

My greatest accomplishments have come as a result of failing and dealing with sometimes harsh consequences. Yet the younger generations seem to experience considerably fewer opportunities to fail because of safety nets, helicopter parents, and last-minute quick fixes to solve problems. For far too many, their branch doesn't creak at all because they have never even climbed the tree. They seldom understand or appreciate the value of struggling, being uncomfortable at times, and earning one's way as a result of merit through tenacious perseverance, courage, and enduring commitment to triumph. These qualities and experiences are the backbone of a life spent making a positive difference for ourselves and the people around us.

After my presentations, I often chat with parents who are extremely frustrated at their inability to motivate their sons or daughters. They report that their children are parked comfortably on the couch lacking the self-motivation to look for a job, attend school, or generally take control over their own lives. Their children do not hear the branch creak because they are too comfortable. They may even feel a sense of entitlement since most amusements and luxuries, not to mention necessities, have been made easily available to them since birth. Developing self-reliance and independence is challenging at this point because dependency and entitlement have taken strong root.

To be candid, the difficulty in many cases lies with parents who have become ineffective at teaching and guiding their children through the stark realities of life. It has been my experience that allowing children to be uncomfortable at times is a positive step toward real growth and understanding. In addition, holding them to time-honored ideals, having realistic and positive expectations, and measuring out sensible and consistent consequences are the key strategies for encouraging character, integrity, purpose, and achievement.

I know a superb, positive, passionate teacher who often comments that parents expect her to not only teach their sons and daughters, but also to rear them by teaching the facts of life, adjusting their behavior, giving them purpose and direction, and inspiring them to self-motivation. She has never actually said this to a parent, but has commented to me on numerous occasions that in one hour per day, she cannot possibly overcome 18 years of poor parenting. But in our school systems today we are asking many of our best and brightest teachers to do exactly that—rear our children. It is unfair to expect teachers and school systems that are already stretched thin on resources to do all the things they are being asked to accomplish. Perhaps it's time to return to the basics: teachers need to teach, and parents need to parent.

I can see the frustration and dismay in the eyes of parents concerning the inability of their sons and daughters to take appropriate action on almost anything. They often state how entitled and special their kids believe they are. I cannot emphasize it enough: the younger generations are exactly the way we made them. In many cases, these traits are a direct result of excessive coddling and an overprotective tendency to make their lives as stress-free as possible.

In far too many examples we, as the older generations, take on their responsibilities in the hope they will thrive as a result—although all too often the opposite is true as they feel even more entitled, comfortable, and unmotivated to achieve their real potential.

But we have an opportunity before us to change our mindset and help unleash the passion, purpose, and performance of today's young people. Employers are looking for the right employees, in the right positions, for the right reasons, and they struggle to unearth the empowered, skilled, passionate team members who will take ownership and responsibility for a job well done, for the good of the organization as well as themselves. Those candidates are out there, but in far too few numbers. The good news is we can help bolster the ranks of qualified people—if we can coach parents to change their approach. Part of this change includes opening their minds to all the different pathways available to their children. Parents are often the most effective voice to bridge the Awareness Gap for their children. But they can't address that gap for their children if it hasn't already been bridged for them.

Bridging the Awareness Gap begins with rethinking the notion that going to college is the only path to a successful career rather than one of the other routes a young person can take in building a successful and fulfilling lifestyle. "We need to overcome what business and industry people call 'the mom factor,'" says Cathie Raymond, who was the CTE director of a successful school district before becoming deputy associate superintendent/state CTE director for Arizona. "Even when someone tells a parent that their kid could make six figures in precision manufacturing, the parent dismisses that as blue-collar work. But we need to reach these parents early on, as soon as elementary school, to get them to realize that college isn't the only viable path to making a good living. Not every child is suitable for college. But that is up to each child to determine for themselves based on their own goals, ambitions, and unique skills, talents, and abilities—far too many students have that choice made for them. At the same time, we need to do a better job at promoting the new face of industry and the potential opportunities young people have available to them there."[3]

A great success story along these lines comes from Jen Schottke, who is the vice president of workforce development for Associated Builders and Contractors (ABC) of Western Michigan. Her role is to help inspire other young people to think about careers in the world of construction—which has been a challenge in the years following the Great Recession that began in 2008. "We went from where is all the work to where are all the people," says Jen, who also happens to be a member of the Why Generation and a mom. Graduates of her Jumpstart Training Program, which is aimed at high schoolers and gives them the basic skills needed on a job site, have a high likelihood of landing at least an entry-level position when they graduate if that's a path they are interested in. Jen told me about one student named Garran who really made an impression on her. Jen visited Garran's class in high school and had the opportunity to talk to him about opportunities in the world of construction—so much more than just digging holes. Jen showed Garran the avenues available that many folks might not know about, such as HVAC, electrical, masonry, and carpentry. Garran was particularly taken by what he heard about masonry—he felt a real connection to the profession even though it was something he had never thought about before. He even got to spend some time with the masonry instructor at the area school, which only stoked his interest further.

Fast forward a few months to what is known as "signing day," when high schoolers can enroll in the program during a ceremony in which they officially commit to the training field of their choice. As you might guess, involving parents of the new recruits is a big part of the event, and Garran's dad attended. At one point, parents get to sit down with administrators and instructors and ask whatever questions they might have about the program. Jen remembers Garran's dad was both inquisitive and challenging. He asked questions such as, "How much do people make?" and "How do you deal with seasonal work?" It was a great opportunity to dispel whatever myths Garran's dad and the other parents had picked up—in other words, to bridge their own Awareness Gap. One of the other parents there happened to work in the construction field, so he served as an unexpected source of information and advocate.

At the end of the event, Garran's dad leaned over to one of the program administrators and said, "This is a big deal. Why don't more people know about this?" In other words, he had shifted from a doubter into a believer about the many pathways his son could take to gain a competitive advantage in today's new economy whether he decided to go to college or not. His Awareness Gap had been bridged.

"We really reshaped that father's mindset about our training program and the industry in general," says Jen. "We're filling the skills gap—one student, educator, and parent at a time. It's really a grassroots effort. But there is no better feeling than when you can shift those mindsets." In addition to her work with ABC, Jen now serves on the school board of her local school system where she is engaging her fellow board members, many of them with PhDs, about the myriad pathways available to students to create the kind of life they want for themselves.[4]

The first step to changing someone's mind is to get them to think bigger than they may have ever done before in their life—which is what finding your Light at the End of the Tunnel is all about.

CHAPTER FOUR INSIGHTS

- It's time for parents to rethink how they can best help their children succeed in today's economy. Often, the younger generations struggle to feel the urgency to become independent and successful adults.

- In general, Why Generation members have not been pushed outside of their comfort zone, so they don't understand why they are not getting what they want out of their lives and careers. They have not learned the value of failure and struggle.

- According to the latest cognitive science research, failure is essential to effective learning. Those who are not allowed to feel they have failed may miss a crucial learning opportunity.

- The parents of the Why Generation have played key roles in shielding their children from making their own choices and experiencing the consequences— something we've taken to calling helicopter parenting. That's understandable to a degree, but it's also creating challenges for their children.

- It's no surprise, then, that so many parents struggle with finding ways to motivate their children to pursue their goals—or even to move out of their basement. On the other end of the parenting spectrum, some young people have experienced a branch creak at too young an age due to neglect or abuse at home. Building hope, showing a strong Light at the End of the Tunnel, and affirming their ability to overcome challenges are especially critical to helping these students thrive.

- Parents can play key roles in bridging the Awareness Gap that exists about how we can better make young people career ready earlier—but first, the gap must be bridged for them. Rather than steering their children only on the college path, they need to become more aware of the vast opportunities available in middle and high school. This will give their kids a competitive edge that makes a powerful difference for both college and every other pathway.

CHAPTER FIVE

Finding the Light at the End of the Tunnel

Goal-setting is an elusive skill for today's youth—and for many adults as well. As an avid goal-setter, I've always understood the tremendous benefits of a clearly defined goal with the frequent reaffirmation of that goal throughout the journey to accomplish it. If you have no goal, any road will get you there.

The Light at the End of the Tunnel is a concept I developed to better understand the relationship between self-motivation and outside motivation when it comes to achieving goals. Self-motivation is what propels us forward in a truly proactive fashion because it is based on our own wants, needs, and desires for a positive outcome. Outside motivation, in many cases, moves us to action in a reactive way due to external forces pushing us one way or another as those influences dictate. With outside motivation, we are less in control and are at the mercy of those forces. Both self-motivation and outside motivation can produce branch creaks in our life. What branch creaks help produce is what I call the "want-to"—and whenever the "want-to" is strong enough, the "how-to" will come.

Think of the tunnel as the work, labor, and effort required to achieve your goals, which are the light at the other end of that tunnel. In order to motivate yourself to go through the tunnel, there must be a powerful light, or "want-to," at the opposite end to entice you sufficiently to persist through the tunnel to reach it. The light represents anything you want. It might be the kind of career, lifestyle, or relationships you want to achieve. Perhaps it is a specific material need or want that has been pent up for some time, or an impulse item that has recently appeared on your radar screen. Perhaps it is a certain position at work, recognition, or personal achievement. However you perceive it, and we all perceive it differently, the light is the reward and therefore the motivation necessary to journey through the tunnel. Understanding this concept is key to motivating both ourselves and others to achieve what we want.

What's the light at the end of your tunnel that motivates you to persevere when things get tough in your life? What's the light for your children, students, employees, and others in your sphere of influence? Understanding the forces that motivate us and others from within is the first step toward harnessing those desires for positive change.

Lessons Learned at Home

I am a single dad of two boys, Matt and Nick, and I have had the joyful and yet formidable task of rearing them since the ages of 14 and 12. I accomplished this while building my company, TFS, to international prominence in the education and workforce development niche we serve. Candidly, there is no greater achievement in my life than being the father of Matt and Nick, who are wonderful young men today in their own right. I am so proud of their accomplishments: they are independent, self-reliant, successful, gainfully employed, and living on their own. I haven't needed to write a check to either of them for many years. I do not take credit for their success, as it truly belongs to them. They navigated challenges that began in childhood and continued through adolescence.

Matt is older than Nick by 22 months, and it is astonishing to me that you can dip into the same gene pool twice and come up with two totally different kids. They are just entering their 30s today, and it is as if Nick looked at Matt at the age of 5 and said, "That just isn't for me." They are both intelligent, but Matt is organized, neat, methodical, and purposeful, while Nick is not even close to pulling those traits off. They are both wonderful young men, but far apart on the "how to live life" spectrum. Neither is right or wrong—just unique in his approach to what makes him comfortable.

Matt was an okay student but didn't have the drive to truly achieve his full potential. Like me, he lacked the vision and desire to be a good student (although in many cases he did better than I did).

Nick, on the other hand, was given the gift of a bright mind capable of capturing information quickly and retaining it for future use. He is smart, resourceful, and in need of constant dynamic challenges or he will tune out and move on. On the other hand, he is not organized and couldn't seem to remember important life logistics such as cleaning up his room (bulldozer needed), performing tasks around the house, or doing his homework.

Much of what I have learned and shared in this book has been verified and punctuated by my sons' journeys. They are the embodiment of the Why Generation in the traits they display in their lives. During their adolescent years, they were nurtured, entitled, and comfortable—far too comfortable. I did not want to be a helicopter parent, constantly hovering over their heads to make sure everything was smooth and easy for them. I knew they needed something different from me if they were ever to experience the personal growth that only comes with facing and solving the difficulties of life.

As my frustration turned into resolve, I noticed that my sons' lack of self-motivation was only rivaled by their overabundance of comfort. We lived in a beautiful house with lots of space, access to high-speed Internet, Wi-Fi, and a large-screen TV with a cutting-edge video game console. We were always sporting the best equipment, latest games, and plenty of audiovisual punch to give realism to any game environment. It was impressive—in fact, too impressive. My sons found relief and escape in that game system—they loved it, and it became the source of much joy and happiness. It also became the reason to put off chores, homework, and schoolwork. It was becoming too powerful in their lives, and that had to change. Frankly, my sons needed to hear the branch creak.

We had rules in our house, and for the most part my sons participated in these rules with only minor exceptions, as they were good kids and knew that ultimately we were in this together. They knew I loved them and that I wanted the best for them—but this translated into a casual view of life as opposed to a focused, determined, and purposeful perspective. If they were going to reach that next step in maturity, they needed to be less comfortable and take ownership of their lives.

Remember, experience is everything to these generations, and my sons were no different. They loved all things tech- and game-related; those were the experiences they gravitated toward with the deepest interest. As a single parent, I struggled early on to ensure that they both studied and worked on their homework. There were too many distractions, though, and they inherited a few too many of my own study habits. These combinations led to poor results and too many stressful discussions about their performance. Something had to change . . . they needed to hear the branch creak.

It was time to shake the branch, so we set firm boundaries in the house about the use of TV and game systems. We created a reward system for performance and tied that to their ability to do the things they wanted to do. These rules were never enforced maliciously, but as a simple part of life. There were things we needed to do and things we liked to do; need always came first. My life became much easier when we established the proper boundaries and tied rewards to performance. There were many days when performance lacked, but so did their ability to do the things they liked to do. Oh, they tested me. They would fall short on performance and still want the reward, but I remained steadfast. At first it was not easy, but as I stayed strong and adhered to the boundaries we set, they eventually came around and accepted how things were. They learned that doing their chores and homework would lead to more of the things they wanted.

And this was just the beginning. The big-picture process of moving them toward maturity started with simple chats about performance requirements, contributions to the family, and long-range goals and objectives. I found the best strategy was to divide and conquer by having a series of simple chats, over time, with each of them individually to convey several key expectations. We spoke candidly about values, performance, and looking for their Light at the End of the Tunnel. I wanted to know what their interests were and how they saw their lives progressing from this point. I wanted to know what they loved to do, what they did well, and how they planned to find the perfect intersection of what they loved to do and the skills, knowledge, and action they were prepared to contribute to achieve their vision.

Something I have learned over the course of my life is that real change starts in our thought life. This was the kind of change I wanted to help my sons experience. I recently had an amazing opportunity to interview best-selling author and international speaker Brian Tracy, one of my motivational heroes. Among the many different topics we discussed, one thing he said struck me the most. It's a motivational strategy I have used in my own life that also describes the recurring conversations I had with Matt and Nick. He said, "If you feed your mind with a particular message, it actually creates new neural grooves and you begin to change your thinking and reaction patterns as well as your emotions. Your brain is not fixed; it is very much malleable—it can actually become reshaped by feeding it continuous, steady streams of new information."[1] By keeping their future at the forefront of their minds, I hoped to help Matt and Nick build new thought patterns and goals as the catalyst for positive change.

I did not expect definitive answers in these early conversations, but I wanted to plant the seeds of self-motivation, vision, and relevance in their performance. I attempted to connect the dots to their future—any future. The one constant you can count on is that these younger generations truly do not know what they do not know—they think they know, but they don't know—you know? As a result of that realization, I saw it as part of my parental job description to start laying the foundation for self-reliance and independence, and these chats were critical to that logical end game.

In my keynote speeches, I cover some of what you are reading in these pages, and I experience two diametrically opposed reactions. First, and most often, I encounter parents who would love to get their older children off the couch, out of the house, and moving toward being self-reliant and independent. These participants thank me for putting new perspective on how they can achieve that result. Second (and significantly less often than the first group), I meet parents who are thrilled their older children are living in their homes and hope they stay there forever. These participants are reacting based on their own emotions and what they perceive as everyone's best interest as opposed to what truly is in the long-term best interest of their children. Simply stated, they like having their children home and permanently connected as part of the normal day-to-day household activity. I can't say that either of these is right or wrong, but the second group averts a key growth opportunity for their children. This growth only comes with their sons and daughters venturing out on their own to earn income, pay taxes, budget effectively, and experience the full freedom of being the captain of their own destiny. This builds a sense of pride, self-satisfaction, and accomplishment that cannot be achieved by adult children living with their parents.

That is what I wanted for my sons. I was determined that my sons would know what they know and act based on that knowledge. I didn't want to kick them out of the house, but I wanted to eliminate the safety net that made life so comfortable, satisfying, and complacent.

I needed a plan like that of Hernán Cortés, who in 1519 ordered the scuttling of his ships once his expedition reached Mexico to ensure that his crew would be motivated to conquer and succeed in this new land. If the ships were in sight, available for a hasty retreat, once the going got tough they would become the easy choice for the crew. He avoided the potential for dissension by destroying the safety net—the ships. He secured his crew's motivation, dedication, and teamwork (as they now each had a vested interest), and ultimately achieved success in their mission. I, too, wanted my sons to be motivated to conquer and succeed in their lives. It was now time to scuttle the ships and create the branch creak they needed to foster self-motivation.

As an essential part of each conversation, we chatted about the remarkable opportunities that life can offer. The vast number of careers, occupations, pathways, and education choices could seem daunting but had to be considered purposefully to achieve the life they wanted to enjoy. We spoke about using their high school years as an opportunity to figure out life, try new things, and explore unique opportunities, clubs, and societies. I understood, as I shared earlier, that if lifestyle is the most important consideration of every Why Generation decision, then lifestyle needed to be an integral part of the decision-making process.

These chats, which started late in their middle school years and continued through high school, were an opportunity for me to plant the seeds necessary to create knowledge, understanding, and motivation. It has been said that when the student is ready, the teacher will appear. I believe that to be true. The knowledge that Matt and Nick were slowly accumulating was not made up of "aha" moments, but rather a gradual drip sequence of understanding that one day would pay off when they saw, experienced, and discerned the right pathway or course of action for their lives. On that day, the teacher would appear, and the gradual building of knowledge would become valued as the road map for the next steps.

Each of those brief chats was fun, enjoyable, and stress free, as it didn't require immediate action that day. I committed to the long game of building a strong root system from the ground up for each of my sons. Harking back to Cortés, it was also important to plant an additional seed to scuttle their ships and help them hear the branch creak for their knowledge, understanding, and potential to become real and one day realized.

To plant that final seed we would chat about experiences in high school and about college, the military, entrepreneurship, and what life might look like and feel like going directly into a career after high school with some kind of certification or license. All of these were possible based on their unique interests, talents, and abilities. I would occasionally then emphasize that on or sometime around August 30 of the year they graduated from high school, they would be moving out to attend college, to serve in the military, to start employment, to live with friends, or to take another worthwhile pathway of their choosing. The common denominator was they were going to be moving out. I scuttled their ship.

I set a hard, firm date where they would be moving out of the nest and living on their own. I didn't do this because I wanted to kick them out; on the contrary, I did this because I love my sons and I felt that for their benefit I had to extricate them from our remarkably comfortable home. I knew my sons would live with me forever if they could watch movies, play video games, and crash on the couch as their whims dictated. It was time to remove that option and help them hear the branch creak beneath their feet. As stated earlier, growth happens when we step outside our comfort zones— almost never when we feel safe and secure.

Candidly, once that seed was planted, it was never a point of contention. They simply accepted they were moving out. They recognized that reality because it was planted years in advance as simply the way life works.

As a result of chatting frequently and establishing ongoing expectations as my sons grew up, we have fostered a rewarding, lifelong adult relationship that is strong, respectful, fulfilling, and fun. We have a wonderful time together, and it is always refreshing to hear the latest updates on what's happening in their lives. In their own ways, they have each affirmed their appreciation for lessons learned, and I can frequently see a deep satisfaction in their accomplishments as they deal with the challenges and inevitable struggles that life can bring. My sons have become increasingly motivated to perform at higher levels, and they truly embrace the responsibility for their own lives. Moreover, as a by-product of that responsibility, they have built significantly more pride in their achievements, which has produced resilient self-esteem—something that cannot be given, but only earned.

I strove to teach my sons that the satisfaction of doing what you love passionately while developing self-reliance and independence is what creates pride in one's own actions. And that healthy pride is what shapes and cultivates an ongoing positive self-esteem. This has to be modeled before it can be taught. When we live it ourselves, our message will have much more credibility with those in our spheres of influence. If the "want-to" is strong enough, the "how-to" will come . . . as it did in our home.

The "Want-to," "How-to" Concept

It has always amazed me how we all can justify, plan, perform remarkably, and achieve astounding results when we put our minds to something. Hands down, the human spirit is one of the most miraculous, problem-solving, and persistent forces in the universe. I have come to believe that almost anything is possible. (I believe this with the slight caveat that I, in no way conceivable, could paint the remarkable ceiling of the Sistine Chapel or discover a cure for polio because I simply was not given the vital skills at birth to accomplish such amazing feats.) Outside those physical and intellectual limitations placed on us from birth or through our DNA, I believe that almost anything is possible when we focus, plan, and take action.

Have you ever wanted something you couldn't afford and within a short amount of time were able to acquire that item or event? I suspect many of us have experienced this. The "want-to" is resilient and creates a strong sense of urgency and desire within our consciousness. We think about that thing we want. We visualize its structure and form. We envision it in our possession and imagine what life would be like with our newly acquired item. Perhaps it makes life easier for us or perhaps it simply looks darn good wrapped around us—like a car, a suit, a gown, or jewelry. We want it. We want to review every angle possible to make it work. We want to leave no stone unturned to accomplish this acquisition goal.

When we arrive at a strong "want-to," the "how-to" takes over and makes things happen for us. There have been many times in my life where my bank account said no, but I was able to trim a little here, cut a chunk there, and find a way to creatively finance my desire. In reality, my "how-to" creatively financed and satisfied my strong "want-to" craving. This pattern works in many ways, and the best life illustration I can use is my son Nick's high school and college experiences.

Nick's Story

School was not really built for Nick. That steady stream of homework, memorization, and sitting still while someone is talking at you was, for him, a prescription for boredom and mischief. Nick has attention deficit disorder (ADD), and his ability to pay attention is roughly equivalent to the time it takes to snap your fingers. This proved challenging in a classroom environment where things moved slowly and the curriculum was rarely geared to take advantage of Nick's strengths. The real problem was that the traditional school setting did not answer his unspoken "why?"

Grammar school was interesting, as we were just beginning to come to grips with Nick's challenges. I didn't even know what ADD was until he was in sixth grade. I will never forget that day because I was called into Nick's sixth-grade principal's office. Nick and I were seated quietly, waiting for the principal to join us, when the door flew open and the principal strolled into the room holding a folder with "Nicholas Perna" inscribed across the top. Oh my, I thought— they have a file.

I stood to shake hands and exchange a moment of pleasantries. The office was big enough for a desk, several chairs, a credenza, and two overfilled bookcases. Nick and I sat across the desk from the principal as he started the meeting. He asked, "Do you have a history of ADD in your family?" I thought, what a silly question, we have always had the ability to add in my family. In fact, why is he spelling this out in front of Nick? He's not stupid; he knows what those letters spell. I asked for clarification, and the principal went on to enlighten me about what ADD is and how it had been negatively affecting Nick through sixth grade. From that time forward, we have been adapting to his need to stay as focused as possible. And it has always been a challenge.

When we were told that Nick had attention deficit disorder, I assumed that meant he could not focus on anything for a long period of time. That was untrue. If he wanted to do something, he could focus on it for hours or even days. I argued about the diagnosis because he could play a video game for six hours, advancing from level to level, while achieving a high score (and avoiding his homework). That was pretty focused in my view. But you see, Nick wanted to play the game—when the "want-to" is strong enough, the "how-to" will come—and he learned how to focus when it was something he wanted to do.

For Nick, high school became a motivating experience, though of course it didn't start out that way. Halfway through his sophomore year, I was discouraged with Nick's performance, as he was sporting an uninspiring 1.5 grade point average (GPA). The frustrating thing was that he aced almost every test. Nick had a 4.0 understanding of everything that was taught to him in high school; he just never turned in homework assignments.

Homework was clearly a nuisance, because he viewed it as irrelevant. In his view, if he got a nearly perfect score on every test, he clearly knew the material, so why should he have to turn in the homework assignments? He would say, "Isn't the goal of school to know the material?" Despite clever logic on his part, I made the pitch about the importance of homework, what it demonstrates, and so on. Nick did try after that, but I had to hound him like a storm trooper to complete his homework. Even when it was completed and visually verified, it would often magically disappear before it was time to hand it in. Some might call him scatterbrained, forgetful, or careless, but it was more than that.

Nick lacked the internal self-motivation necessary to complete those assignments and ensure they made it safely to school. There was no light, no "want-to," no valid reason to succeed and devote the appropriate effort. Sure, it was important to me, his teacher, and the school, but it was clearly not important enough to *him* to take real action.

Throughout most of his sophomore year, Nick lived a dad-driven life. He did most things because the request came from me or because of a rule I had established. He played along the best he could but viewed the activities as work and effort for which he did not see the payoff or Light at the End of the Tunnel. This can be demonstrated by Nick's attendance records for his freshman and sophomore years. He missed the maximum number of days each year, and I had to scramble both years to find doctor's notes because we had exceeded the limit of excused absences.

He woke up countless school mornings with excuses to stay home that particular day. He was remarkably creative and convincing with his elaborate collection of reasons. For example, he was frequently nauseated in the mornings and could throw up on cue (that's impressive). Once I was making tea and he sneaked down to the teapot, held a thermometer over it, and then showed me his temperature—105.4°. It was fun to watch him squirm under my response after that experience, but he did earn an A+ for effort and creativity. Quite simply, he did not like school because he was not engaged, it was boring, and there was no Light at the End of the Tunnel for him.

Midway through his sophomore year, on a structured field trip, Nick visited Cuyahoga Valley Career Center (CVCC), located 20 minutes south of Cleveland, Ohio. It is a facility focused on educating and training students in a myriad of high-tech career fields.

Nick toured the buildings along with the rest of the sophomore class, little knowing that his life would be transformed the moment he walked into the programming and software development area. Nick has always been a big-time geek and nerd. I know that might sound insulting because when I grew up, geeks and nerds carried a negative stereotype—but not today. Being called a geek or nerd is a respectful badge of honor.

Nick the geek was now standing in a place where geeks and nerds work, hang out, and talk all things nerdy, all the time. For the first time in Nick's education experience, he saw the possibility of liking school. This was the missing piece; this was the answer why. He saw a place where he could fit in. The teacher addressed the group and started talking nerd talk to the visitors . . . and Nick was home. Nick decided on the spot that this was what he wanted to do with his life. The Light at the End of the Tunnel blazed into his consciousness, and the "want-to" necessary to achieve it was in the early stages of taking over.

As I described earlier, this strategy proved effective on that momentous day when Nick learned about programming and software development. He celebrated that he knew what he wanted to be in his life—a software engineer. On that day the drip sequence of chats paid off. It's possible he may not have recognized that opportunity had he not known that at some point he would need to become the captain of his own ship and journey beyond the nest to find his own way. That healthy sense of urgency drove him to become self-motivated and achieve at a significantly higher level once he had direction and recognized his own Light at the End of the Tunnel when it blazed for him.

The branch creaked for Nick the moment he created the "want-to" for something better. He found himself eager to get started, so he focused, planned, and took action. He was about to venture far beyond his comfort zone and test his capacity for growth in his life.

It wouldn't be easy, but he was prepared to do whatever was necessary to achieve his Light at the End of the Tunnel.

At this moment, Nick went from living a dad-driven life to a Nick-driven life.

The Nick-Driven Life

It's a beautiful thing to witness someone finally seeing the Light at the End of the Tunnel in his life—it changes everything. The Nick-driven life looked altogether different from the dad-driven life. As Nick took control of his life with his scope locked on what he wanted—the Light at the End of the Tunnel—he started to make plans for how to spend his life doing programming and software development.

He researched the program he wanted to take, the colleges where he would continue his studies, and the jobs and incomes available upon completion of college and his ascendancy into the workforce. He was pumped, and I was thrilled that he finally found what he had been missing all along: the passion and purpose that lead to greater performance.

Nick's Light at the End of the Tunnel was a profitable and successful career as a programming guru with the fun, nerdy lifestyle to match. He was excited, happy, and dare I say, motivated. The "want-to" was now in full control of Nick's future. He knew what he wanted, but he had many obstacles to overcome. For starters, Nick needed better grades to get to college because a 1.5 GPA was not going to make the cut. In order to get better grades Nick could no longer miss school and was going to have to turn in homework.

Miraculously, that is exactly what happened. Nick with his newfound "want-to" discovered "how-to" turn things around. It's one of the key insights of this book: if the "want-to" is strong enough, the "how-to" will come. Well, he figured out "how-to" complete and turn his homework assignments in on time, show up for classes, not miss school, and dig himself out of the hole he had created during his freshman and sophomore years.

The outcome was impressive. Nick finished high school with a significantly higher GPA, missed only two days each of his last two years, scored high on the ACT test, and after earning a small scholarship entered the University of Akron to obtain a BS in computer science. From there he kept his eyes focused on the Light at the End of the Tunnel as he completed his degree in computer science, graduated UA, and was offered two programming positions starting at $48,000 per year in the Cleveland area doing exactly what he wanted to do. He selected one of the offers and now lives nearby, makes great money, and truly enjoys what he does. He is always talking about the next steps and opportunities available to him as he progresses upward in his career.

I am remarkably proud of what he has accomplished by refocusing his life toward productive pursuits while at the same time satisfying his desire to do something he loves. We should all be so lucky. And yet it wasn't just luck, was it?

I cringe when I think what might have happened to Nick if he had not had the opportunity to discover his dream back in his sophomore year of high school—if he hadn't been fortunate enough to explore his interests and determine at an early age what he wanted to do with his life. I wish I could say all his success was possible because of my outstanding parenting skills, but the credit goes to the Light at the End of the Tunnel that Nick saw and the "want-to" it created in his life. Once that happened, I simply had to get out of his way and allow him to make the self-motivated decisions for his life based on the outcome he wanted.

The Light at the End of the Tunnel is a critical strategy to help each of us develop the "want-to" that fosters self-motivation, achievement, and positive self-esteem. For those teaching and mentoring others, it has multiple applications in the classroom, workplace, and home—especially when those young people are given a menu of options to choose from. Or, to think about it a different way, it's a way for them to think about the different branches they might be excited to climb out on.

It's my belief that when it comes to making a living, we only do one of three things. Number one, we have a job—this describes the type of work that feels like drudgery or a dead end. We don't love it, we may not even like it—we just do it because we have to. Most people have experienced this at some point in their working lives. Number two, we build a career—this is a role where we feel driven to succeed and do our work well. But it's still laborious at times. The third option is to pursue a mission. This is where work doesn't feel like work because we are doing something we are passionate about, something we believe in. Our "want-to" fuels the "how-to" so strongly that we look forward to performing the tasks and projects that achieve our vision. Pursuing a mission in our professional lives transcends both the drudgery of a mere job and the commitment to a career because it's bigger than the income or status that comes with the position. It's a purposeful lifework where we enjoy the perfect intersection of work and lifestyle and feel we are making a positive difference in the world.

I should be quick to add: pursuing a mission in your professional life looks different for everyone. What would be an uninspiring or even tedious job for one person could easily be a passion-driven calling for someone with different talents, skills, and abilities. The key is discovering what you love to do and pursuing it passionately as the mission that drives your purpose.

For what it's worth, whenever I share Nick's story to illustrate these concepts, I almost always hear from someone that "I have a Nick at home" or "I have a Nick in my classroom." Do you?

Building Your Dream

In a successful speaking career that has largely focused on addressing educators, employers, and community organizations, I had never branched out to speak directly to students or employees. That all changed when I heard the branch creak with an invitation to speak to high school career and technical education ambassador students in Arizona. I suppose it was about time to focus, plan, and put my concepts in front of the end users of so many of my strategies.

I titled my speech "Living the Dream." And it was, to my sheer delight, remarkably well received. This was my opportunity to start with a drip and see how far the ripples could travel with young and energetic teenagers who had their entire lives ahead of them. I started by asking a series of questions that got students immediately engaged, raising their hands in participation. These were simple questions such as, "How many of you love to take vacations? Go to movies? Attend concerts? How many of you would like to do those things as an adult?" At each question almost every hand flew up with great excitement. Yes! Yes! Yes!

The last question was, "How many of you want to live the dream?" The hands flew up and then backed down slightly as the questions shot up at me: "What do you mean by living the dream? Whose dream? What dream?" Exactly! We live in a world where success seems easy and attainable on TV and in movies, but what really constitutes "the dream" . . . not just for the students that day but for each of us regardless of our age? Is the dream financial independence? Perhaps for some. Is it doing what you want, when you want? Perhaps. Is it living where you want and with whom you want? Why not? In the final analysis the dream is whatever you want it to be for you personally.

I challenged each student to seek out their unique dream, desire for their life, and Light at the End of the Tunnel. The sooner you determine your course, the faster you arrive at your destination.

Discover what you are passionate about and what inspires you, and realistically evaluate the strengths and weaknesses associated with your own abilities. Build your dream. They were all in.

I then shared a perspective that has driven me for most of my adult life. I shared a story about how I had my own personal employment branch creak shortly after graduating from college. I came to a powerful realization as I was 60 days from losing my first adult job. I realized that, along with focusing, planning, and taking action, we really only do two things in this world: we are either building our dream or building someone else's. That's it. It's that simple.

I came to ask myself: every time I watched TV, went to a movie, or attended a performance—whose dream was I building? Yes, that of the studios, actors, producers, and others. Whose dream was I building when I watched a sporting event? That of the well-paid athletes, owners, and TV networks. Whose dream was I building when I put my money down for a video game, played it all night for two weeks, and invested my hard-earned dollars in online gaming fees? Yes, you get the picture. I was building the dreams of the entire group associated with that game, movie, or sporting event.

This meant I had to be conscious of how I spent my time. There was nothing wrong with building someone else's dream, going to movies, watching sports, or playing video games as long as I carved out a significant amount of time to build my own dream as well. Building my own dream became more important than building someone else's. That awareness allowed me to focus, plan, and take action in my life and has led me to the success I enjoy today. Today I am living my dream as I set out to do many years ago—I run a successful and well-respected business, speak internationally, and travel extensively for both business and pleasure. I interact with and influence a great many people, and I enjoy the time I spend with my family, friends, clients, and coworkers at TFS who share my vision for transforming education and workforce development nationwide. I take great pleasure in various hobbies and interests, and I have cultivated a genuine passion for making a difference on a grand scale.

That day in Arizona, I encouraged each student to carve out the crucial time to focus, plan, and take action to build his or her own dream, regardless of what the dream, pathway, or Light at the End of the Tunnel was for them. I advised them that their generation spends entirely too much of their priceless time building other people's dreams and not nearly enough on developing their own opportunities.

The good news, however, is that they, like Nick, can take control and choose the kind of life they want to build for themselves.

CHAPTER FIVE INSIGHTS

- The key to helping young people reach their goals is to find the sweet spot where they find their own internal motivation to pursue a goal—something I call the Light at the End of the Tunnel.

- Parents can start with simple chats with their children to plant the seeds of growth, goal-setting, and personal responsibility.

- The power of the "want-to, how-to" concept is that when a young person establishes the desire to do something, it becomes much easier to figure out and take the "how-to" steps to reach the destination.

- Too often we wait until after college to challenge a young person with the question of what they want to do with their life. But, as Nick's story illustrates for us, we can and should begin this process and exploration much earlier.

- When young people find their internal motivation, they also learn to take control of their own lives— which is incredibly inspiring to see in action.

- We should encourage young people to build their own dream and seek out their personal Light at the End of the Tunnel rather than investing all their time in other people's dreams.

CHAPTER SIX

Bridging the Awareness Gap

One day in late 2014 I delivered a dynamic speech to a large, fully engaged, and interactive audience made up of college and high school career and technical administrators, teachers, and critical support staff. I spoke passionately about how they could significantly increase performance in the younger generations by helping them hear the branch creak in their lives. I shared how generating the "want-to" is associated with students finding their own Light at the End of the Tunnel based on their unique interests, talents, and abilities. Success for these younger generations comes with their personal discovery of that perfect intersection of career and lifestyle.

The speech went well, and I received an enthusiastic ovation at the end of the presentation (always appreciated). Afterward, I greeted a great number of people who had formed a line to one side of the stage, but one individual stood out from all the rest. He was a teacher that I guessed to be in his mid-50s. When he spoke, his deep, slightly raspy voice commanded attention. When he approached, he was not nearly as enthusiastic as the other folks in line. He introduced himself and proceeded to tell me that he thought all this information regarding the younger generations, creating the "want-to," and blazing the Light at the End of the Tunnel was interesting, but that "these kids" (that's how he referred to them) "do not know the first thing about what they want to do with their lives—they are totally clueless."

I wish I could tell you that he delivered that statement in a matter-of-fact way . . . but he didn't. He said it coldly, abruptly, and with a spattering of anger and frustration that stopped me in my tracks. He was serious and deliberate, as though he had harbored these thoughts for far too long and was now prepared to launch a diatribe at an unsuspecting recipient—me. I listened and tried to understand his concerns with the younger generations, but ultimately left the conversation unable to influence his perspective on what he unquestionably experiences in his teaching position. Not knowing anything else about the gentleman, I can only speculate that he teaches a challenging group of students who see no Light at the End of the Tunnel and have no "want-to" that drives their action. My sons went through this period as well, and it wasn't easy. He must be dealing with that at every turn to have made his comments with such visible frustration.

I spent the better part of the next several weeks thinking about this man and his heartbreaking perspective on our younger generations. Can it be true that "these kids do not know the first thing about what they want to do with their lives" and that "they are totally clueless"? Certainly a great many young people today do not know what they want out of their lives—isn't that buried somewhere in the definition of being young and immature? As I pondered the question, I began to consider that, in the end, he was blaming the students for not knowing what they wanted to do with their own lives.

I thought about that for a while and this reality struck me: students today do not know what they do not know. This is the Awareness Gap I've mentioned earlier, and it's huge in the arena of career exploration. They think they know, but they don't. They have not been shown what's possible and how to get there . . . because we haven't told them. That led me to a simple "aha" moment as I juxtaposed students today who do not know what they do not know and my son Nick, who clearly did not know what he didn't know until the day he returned home, during his sophomore year of high school, from that tour of the career center and declared his aspiration to become a software engineer. I've shared his story; after that visit, Nick suddenly knew what he knew (his "want-to") and was willing to take action to achieve his Light at the End of the Tunnel. He became motivated, passionate, and singularly focused on accomplishing his goal. As I said before, once he saw his light he began living a Nick-driven life. If Nick could make that mental and emotional transition in one day, so could others. So how can we help young people come to their own realization of the Light at the End of the Tunnel for their own lives? How can we effectively tell them what they don't know? How can we support them in their transformation?

But the Awareness Gap is not something only students experience. I am convinced that the parents of today's young people are also unaware of the majority of fulfilling, high-demand, high-wage careers that can be attained by postsecondary training pathways beyond the traditional college route. If the parents don't have a grasp of the full range of possibilities and choices out there, how can they share all those options with their sons and daughters?

There has to be a way to increase awareness among students and parents of the multitude of rewarding careers and occupations that exist in America today. We can turn to school systems for help, but too many teachers, counselors, and administrators are themselves unaware of the robust opportunities available to today's youth because we have devalued career exploration for the sake of sending everyone through one pathway—college.

To change the paradigm, we must help students start at a younger age to make career connections and begin the dialogue about what's possible. Student self-exploration can begin through the plethora of free online tools and resources such as career interest inventories. Many districts today even pay for students to access specialized career interest sites. But at the same time, many within the school system may not know these resources exist, or if they do know, don't fully appreciate the value of these powerful tools to bring focus and purpose to a student's education. These sites support students as they explore and identify their key interests and narrow those down to potential career fields of interest. Students can start using these tools as an introduction to career exploration as early as elementary and middle school during designated times incorporated as a regular part of the classroom schedule, preparing them for more in-depth career exploration and goal-setting in high school. By making earlier career exploration a priority in K–12 settings, students will be equipped to research and pursue viable opportunities and ultimately make much better career and education choices moving forward.

Our goal should be to close the Awareness Gap by conveying the broad range of careers and occupations available to young people today. Whatever strategy we use, it has to tell a compelling success story that the student can see himself in. It has to help change the education paradigm in this country so that we move students toward true career readiness rather than exclusively toward college readiness. It has to demonstrate the expanded options and opportunities that come by exploring career direction in high school rather than waiting until college. It has to capture the imagination of our young people and provide ongoing motivation to keep pushing toward the goals they set based on their own unique interests, talents, and abilities.

The strategic tool I want to share here, the **Career Tree®**, is a powerful illustration of this book's focus on goal-setting and exploration in the classroom.

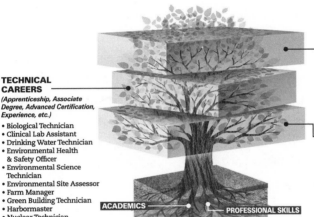

PROFESSIONAL CAREERS
(Bachelor's, Master's, PhD, Specialized Training, Experience, etc.)

- Climatologist
- Clinical Research Associate
- Design Engineer
- Environmental Engineer
- Food Scientist
- Geoscientist
- Marine Biologist
- Meteorologist
- Microbiologist
- Pharmaceutical Sales
- Veterinarian
- Wildlife Biologist

TECHNICAL CAREERS
(Apprenticeship, Associate Degree, Advanced Certification, Experience, etc.)

- Biological Technician
- Clinical Lab Assistant
- Drinking Water Technician
- Environmental Health & Safety Officer
- Environmental Science Technician
- Environmental Site Assessor
- Farm Manager
- Green Building Technician
- Harbormaster
- Nuclear Technician
- Veterinary Technician
- Wastewater Technician

ENTRY-LEVEL CAREERS
(with Program Completion)

- CMP Cleanup Technician
- Equipment Prep Technician
- Farmer
- Field Technician
- Global Information Systems Technician
- Hazardous Waste Response Associate
- Manufacturing Technician
- Nursery Technician
- Rancher
- Site Surveyor
- Solar Sales Associate
- Watershed Science Technician

ACADEMICS — PROFESSIONAL SKILLS
EXPERIENCES — PASSION

BIOTECHNOLOGY

The Career Tree is a refreshing alternative to hundreds of pathways, ladders, flow charts, and other complex metaphors and diagrams that have made education challenging for the layperson to understand. It was born from my work with educators and employers to address our national branch creak caused by the expanding skills gap, rising college costs, and lack of performance on the part of the younger generations—everything we have been discussing in this book up to this point. The Tree is an illustration that distills all of the strategies, generational information, and knowledge into a simple solution for students at any level of education and in any type of school to create their own pathway to a successful life and career.

There may be many different ideas and solutions that meet these pressing needs, but the Career Tree is the culmination of all my research, concepts, and strategies on how to impact young people nationwide. I share this not to impress you but to impress upon you that connecting the dots and taking positive action can produce impressive results with young people. You may have formulated your own concepts based on what has already been discussed—that's great; take action on your ideas to move young people to greater performance. Look beyond the following Career Tree example to the underpinning concept of why it works and why it moves young people to action and greater performance.

Watching Nick find his personal Light at the End of the Tunnel was the kernel of the idea that slowly came to life as I pondered the Awareness Gap so roughly described by that teacher I met back in 2014. Since its inception, the Career Tree has been the most sought-after best practice and response-producing highlight in my keynote addresses. It can also be adapted to the needs of employers by motivating employees to envision—and start achieving—the career possibilities and levels open to them within the company.

Besides its application in the workplace, the Career Tree is designed to be used in any classroom and any area of study. It has been used in academic classrooms as well as career and technical education programs and training centers to start and foster an ongoing dialogue with students and trainees about what careers and occupations are right for them based on their own unique interests, talents, and abilities. They research careers and occupations available in the field of their technical program that look appealing and then the lifestyle associated with that career or occupation. As they do this, their Awareness Gap is bridged, bringing them that much nearer to discovering their own Light at the End of the Tunnel. When they discover the position that hits their personal ideal intersection of career and lifestyle, they write their name and career choice on a Career Leaf label and place it on a full-color, customized, interactive Career Tree wall graphic displayed in their classroom. The moment they affix their Career Leaf to the Tree, it becomes a goal and aspiration. As with the frequent recalibration used in setting effective goals in any area of life, students can change their minds at any time during the ongoing dialogue that is conducted throughout the program of study.

What follows is an example of a career and technical education program, but the possibilities of the Career Tree are truly expandable to all areas of education. Many K–12 school districts, for example, are now embracing the Career Tree for academic pathways such as chemistry, physics, math, biology, and more. Helping students see the relevance—the why—of these academic disciplines to their career and life aspirations will improve performance at every level. Motivation matters, and that is what the Career Tree inspires. It's a win-win for everyone—the students, the parents, the school district, and ultimately our communities, our economy, and our country.

It probably won't surprise you that the Career Tree looks like one of those majestic trees I climbed as a young explorer in my early days. Imagine a proud, sturdy trunk leading up to an expansive and robust branch system filled with seemingly endless possibilities. The trunk of the Career Tree represents the program or course of study that a student has selected. The branch system represents all the careers and occupations that are possible as a result of completing that program or course of study, regardless of the amount of additional education needed to reach any particular branch.

In the early months of crafting the Career Tree strategy, I discussed the concept with over 150 professional college and high school career and technical education teachers nationwide. I asked each of them how many branches (careers and occupations) would be possible as a result of completing their program, regardless of the amount of additional education or training that might be necessary to reach specific branches. The most common reply I heard was that "hundreds of careers and occupations are possible." That's a number that clearly shows the expanding options and opportunities available to students as a result of completing career-focused training as part of a well-rounded education.

The Career Tree concept and strategies are proprietary, trademarked, and copyrighted to ensure that the Career Trees will look and function the same no matter where they are implemented. In addition to the Career Tree image itself, my team has created collateral materials, including a curriculum guide, classroom materials, videos, an online portal, and more—all of which carry a consistent look and message that will ultimately raise the awareness level on a national scale.

The branch system of the Tree is split into three equal horizontal sections. The first level, nearest the trunk, is the "Entry-Level Careers," representing all the careers and occupations that are unlocked immediately following completion of the program of study, or trunk. "Entry-Level" is not synonymous with "low paying," as many can earn a viable living wage depending on the industry and program of study. The term simply refers to the kinds of careers and occupations that are possible right away without any additional education, training, certifications, or licensure required.

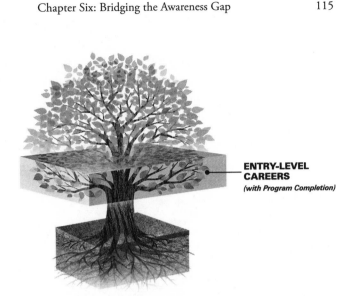

The middle third of the branch system is called the "Technical Careers," which represent all the careers and occupations that students can unlock by obtaining further education such as advanced certifications, apprenticeship completion, specialized training, or a two-year associate degree. In some cases, this level and all its opportunities can also be unlocked through enough work experience and time at the Entry-Level section of the Tree.

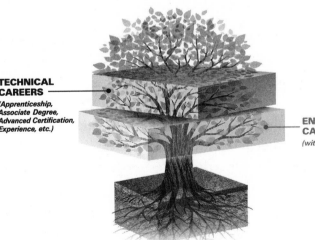

The top third of the branch system is called the "Professional Careers." This level represents all the careers and occupations that are unlocked by obtaining further education, such as a four-year baccalaureate degree, a master's degree, a PhD, or some type of specialized training. In some cases, this level also can be unlocked through enough work experience and time at the Technical Careers section of the Tree.

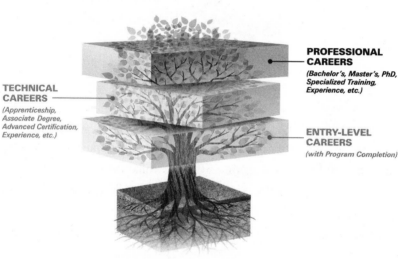

TECHNICAL CAREERS
(Apprenticeship, Associate Degree, Advanced Certification, Experience, etc.)

PROFESSIONAL CAREERS
(Bachelor's, Master's, PhD, Specialized Training, Experience, etc.)

ENTRY-LEVEL CAREERS
(with Program Completion)

It's important to note that I use the term *unlock* in each section because it is illustrative of the way the younger generations think. Have you ever seen a young person play a video game—and how hard they will work to unlock the next level? The Career Tree uses that same strategy, as it visually demonstrates all the possibilities at each level. The student can then indicate the point on the Tree that fits their perfect intersection of career and lifestyle aspirations. To achieve that desired position or goal, they must now unlock that section of the Tree. The "want-to" was just born, and with it the "how-to."

The only difference between the three sections is the amount of education or work experience it takes to ascend to the next level. There is no direct correlation between salary and position on the Tree. The idea that you automatically make more money as you move up the Tree or that your lifestyle is necessarily better the higher you go isn't true. Moving to a new level simply means that you unlock those careers and occupations, but there is no guarantee that it's any better—because every person's definition of "better" is unique. As an illustration of that fact, to become an electrical engineer, someone would need to unlock the Professional Careers section of the Electrical Career Tree with at least a four-year degree or higher. If another person wanted to become an electrician, he or she would need to unlock the Technical Careers section by completing an apprenticeship started in the Entry-Level Careers area of the Tree. Here's the kicker: most people are not aware that in many parts of this country, an electrician can make up to twice as much as an electrical engineer while amassing virtually no educational or training debt along the way.

Both careers are viable, living-wage careers with amazing potential for the individual with enough passion to excel at either one . . . but in this country we tend to look more favorably on the college graduate despite the fact that both avenues are rewarding and vital to our communities and way of life. This example is played out in many industries. Students in both middle and high schools need to be made aware of these possibilities much earlier, enabling them to make the selections that are best suited to their unique interests, talents, and abilities. This allows them to invest wisely in the career, lifestyle, and results they want to attain for their own priorities.

Real-Life Career Trees

An illustration that brings this idea into clear focus is the general high school automotive program available nationwide in many comprehensive high schools, unified school districts, career centers, and more. It is a program that is prevalent, yet most of the public does not truly understand the true competitive advantage that it can deliver to anyone interested in any type of job in the automotive industry.

I have worked with a tremendous number of automotive teachers nationwide who are, many times, keen professionals extremely proud of their industry and how they positively impact students every day. When asked, "What is the greatest misconception and fear that parents have about their son or daughter taking your automotive program?" their answer is always the same: parents are afraid it will turn their son or daughter into a mere "grease monkey." When asked if that is the case, they always answer with a resounding "No!"

In today's competitive automotive environment, cars have become high-tech devices that will one day drive themselves with an impressive array of sensors, computers, and artificial intelligence programs. That may sound frightening, but it's accurate. Completing an automotive program can lead to ASE certification, a vital industry credential that allows the program alumnus to unlock the Entry-Level Careers section of the Automotive Career Tree. The program itself is the trunk of the Tree and leads to the many careers and occupations available as a result of completing the program and becoming ASE certified.

The Entry-Level Career branches of just one school's Automotive Career Tree are illustrated next, as shared with me by professionals in the field. This is an actual Career Tree in use today in this school's automotive program. It's crucial to note that my team doesn't choose the careers that appear on each Tree; teachers get to create their own program or classroom narrative by selecting the most meaningful careers and occupations for their unique program. The instructors decide what is most relevant and viable to create a dialogue with students. Due to the space constraints of the wall graphic that displays these career branches, this is only a partial list of what students can unlock upon completing the program:

- General Service Technician

- Quick Lube/Oil Change Technician

- Tire Service Technician

- Custom Detailer

- Parts Counter Salesperson

- Car Sales Representative

- Customer Service Representative

- Muffler/Brake Service Technician

- Automotive Assembly Technician

- Automotive Parts Recycler

- Automotive Technician Apprentice

- Vehicle Customizer

Rather more options than becoming a grease monkey, aren't there?

The middle third of the Tree, the Technical Careers, is unlocked through further education such as advanced certifications, apprenticeship completion, specialized training, or a two-year associate degree. In some cases, this level can also be unlocked through enough work experience and time spent at the Entry-Level Careers section of the Tree. Next is one school's list of the branches, again chosen by the instructors, located in the Technical Careers section of the Tree:

- Automotive Certified Technician

- Specialty Shop Technician

- High Performance Engine Builder

- Service Shop Manager

- Insurance Adjuster

- Independent Automotive Technician

- Dealer Service Advisor

- Diagnostician

- Race Team/Crew Chief

- Automatic Transmission Technician

- Automotive Restoration Specialist

- Experienced Automotive Detailer

The top third of the Tree, the Professional Careers, is unlocked through further education such as a four-year baccalaureate degree, a master's degree, a PhD, or some sort of specialized training. Again, in some cases this level can be unlocked through enough work experience and time at the Technical Careers section of the Tree. Below is a partial list of the branches the program instructors chose to populate the Professional Careers section of this school's Tree:

- Master Certified Technician

- Automotive Engineer

- Automotive Designer

- Master Engine Builder

- NASCAR Pit Crew Member

- Performance Race Team Technician

- Automotive Research Engineer

- Electronic Aftermarket Specialist

- Automotive Service Shop Owner

- Dealership Owner

- Specialty Shop Owner

- Alternative Fuel Engineer

These careers and occupations are tremendous prospects for the students who love cars and see themselves in the automotive industry where there are many viable, living-wage careers available at every level of the Tree.

But don't mistake the fact that the Career Tree can unlock potential branches in a multitude of sectors and industries. Here's an example of what a Career Tree might look like in the **art** and **performing arts** world:

ENTRY-LEVEL CAREERS

- Tour Guide
- Road Crew, Stage Crew
- Makeup Assistant
- Costume Assistant
- Model, Actor, Dancer
- TV/Radio Voiceover Narrator

- Production Assistant
- Casting Assistant
- Box Office Sales Assistant
- Office Assistant
- Social Media Assistant
- Radio Announcer

TECHNICAL CAREERS

- Concierge
- Volunteer Coordinator
- Stunt Man
- Junior Agent
- Media Technician
- Concert Promoter

- Event Planner
- Project Coordinator
- Makeup Artist
- Technician—Theater, Lighting, Sound
- Marketing Designer
- Publicist

PROFESSIONAL CAREERS

- Illustrator
- Teacher, Professor
- Sign Language Interpreter
- Arts Manager
- Art Museum Curator
- Agent

- Choreographer
- Director
- Producer
- Composer
- Costume Designer
- Set Designer

Or how about an example of a Career Tree in the **education** field?

ENTRY-LEVEL CAREERS

- Youth Development Leader
- Teacher's Aide
- Library Assistant
- Administrative Assistant
- Children's Entertainer
- Family Child Care Provider

- Coach, Sports Instructor
- Camp Counselor
- Party Planner
- Cruise Ship Activity Director
- Party Planner
- Personal Care Aide

TECHNICAL CAREERS

- Child Development Paraprofessional
- Preschool Teacher
- Camp Coordinator
- Child Care Center Director
- Recreation Department Director
- Children's Museum Educator

- Program Planner, Event Planner
- Childcare—Preschool, Head Start, Tutor
- Early Intervention Program Aide
- Corporate Trainer
- Author, Illustrator
- Developmental Specialist

PROFESSIONAL CAREERS

- Teacher, Professor
- Provost, Dean, Superintendent
- Principal, Vice Principal, Dean of Students
- Guidance Counselor
- School Psychologist, Counselor, Nurse

- Therapist—Speech, Occupational, Physical
- Curriculum Specialist
- Library Media Specialist
- Child Psychologist
- Museum Curator
- Camp Director
- Head Start Administrator

You can even create a Career Tree for students to better understand the opportunities in exploring the world of **county government** and **law**:

ENTRY-LEVEL CAREERS

- Elected Official
- Auto Title Assistant
- Board of Election Assistant

- Regional Planning Assistant
- Real Estate Assistant

- Building and Code Assistant
- Dog Shelter Assistant
- Jobs and Family Services Assistant
- Law Librarian

- Children's Services Assistant
- Veterans' Services Assistant
- Wastewater Division Assistant

TECHNICAL CAREERS

- Court Stenographer
- Security Officer
- Building Maintenance Supervisor
- Dog Warden
- Paralegal
- Legal Secretary

- Nutritionist Assistant
- Sheriff Deputy
- Jail Administrator
- Caseworker Assistant
- Parks Maintenance Supervisor
- Solid Waste Education Specialist

PROFESSIONAL CAREERS

- Auditor
- Judge, Magistrate
- Prosecutor, Attorney
- Coroner
- Court IT System Analyst
- Civil Engineer
- Sanitarian

- Emergency Manager
- Health Commissioner
- Human Resource Director
- Controller
- Jobs and Family Services Director

Here's what a Career Tree for the **health science** field looks like:

ENTRY-LEVEL CAREERS

- State-Tested Nurse Assistant
- Patient Care Assistant

- Hospitality Aide
- Dietary Aide
- Home Health Aide

- Resident Care Assistant
- Bill Clerk, Ward Clerk
- Appointment Scheduler
- Health Information Clerk

- Lab Technician Assistant
- Medical Office Receptionist
- Medical Assistant

TECHNICAL CAREERS

- Pharmacy Technician
- Licensed Practical Nurse
- Registered Nurse
- Occupational Therapy Assistant
- Physical Therapy Assistant
- Respiratory Therapist

- Phlebotomist
- Healthcare Technician
- EMT/ Paramedic
- Therapy Aide
- Billing and Coding Specialist
- Massage Therapist

PROFESSIONAL CAREERS

- Speech and Language Pathologist
- Nurse Practitioner
- Nurse Midwife
- Nurse Anesthetist
- Mortician
- Surgeon

- Licensed Social Worker
- Pharmacist
- Medical Doctor
- Dietitian
- Forensic Scientist
- Pediatrician

Have you ever considered how many different positions are available for someone who studies **filmmaking** and **video production**?

ENTRY-LEVEL CAREERS

- Cable TV Camera Operator
- Cable TV Floor Director

- Wedding Camera Operator
- Wedding Video Editor

- Production Assistant
- Slate Operator
- Grip
- Assistant Editor

- Audio Technician
- Cable Wrangler
- Script Assistant
- VFX Assistant

TECHNICAL CAREERS

- Short Film Director
- Short Film Producer
- Cable TV Director
- Cable TV Producer
- Cable TV Technical Director
- Cable TV Sports Replay

- Key Grip
- Best Boy
- Editor
- VFX Artist
- Foley Artist
- Script Writer

PROFESSIONAL CAREERS

- Feature Film Director
- Feature Film Producer
- Network TV Director
- Network TV Producer
- Network TV Camera Operator
- Network TV Technical Director

- Director of Photography
- Gaffer
- Colorist
- VFX Supervisor
- Audio Supervisor
- Script Supervisor

For someone who pursues skills in the field of **math**, here's what their career options might look like:

ENTRY-LEVEL CAREERS

- Cashier
- Stock Person
- Waiter
- Salesperson

- Jr. Data Analyst
- Logistics Advanced Supply Chain Assistant
- Office Manager

- Customer Service
- Apprentice Electrician
- Designer

- Bank Teller
- Math Tutor

TECHNICAL CAREERS

- Industrial Design Technologist
- Packaging Designer
- Home Improvement, Builder
- Construction Worker
- Tool and Die Maker
- Master Flooring Installer
- Surveyor

- Business Owner, Manager
- Research Analyst
- Inventory Analyst
- Geographic and Land Information Systems Analyst
- Air Traffic Control Analyst

PROFESSIONAL CAREERS

- Actuary
- Teacher, Professor
- Accounts Receivable Manager, Accounts Payable Manager
- Statistician, Logistician
- CPA
- CEO

- Financial Advisor
- Physicist
- Engineer—Robotics, Civil, Geomatics
- Economist
- Risk Management Specialist
- CFO

Or how about all the different jobs you can qualify for by pursuing the field of **sports medicine** and **personal training**:

ENTRY-LEVEL CAREERS

- Personal Trainer
- Gym/Club Employee
- Medical Office Employee

- Medical Receptionist
- Physical Therapy Aide
- Sports Coach

- Nutrition Sales Person
- Athletic Programs Supervisor
- Umpire, Referee

- Occupational Therapy Aide
- Child Care Worker
- Fitness Director

TECHNICAL CAREERS

- Physical Therapy Assistant
- Medical Technician
- Surgical Technician
- Medical Assistant
- Radiologic Technician
- Sports Manager

- Respiratory Therapist
- Massage Therapist
- Pilates and Yoga Instructor
- Group Fitness Instructor
- Pharmacy Technician
- Biomedical Equipment Technician

PROFESSIONAL CAREERS

- Medical Doctor
- Physical Therapist
- Athletic Trainer
- Exercise Physiologist
- Physical Education Instructor, Coach
- College Professor

- Forensic Scientist
- Medical Engineer, Biomedical Engineer
- Physician Assistant
- Sports Psychologist
- Sports Nutritionist
- Chiropractor

Finally, here's what the Career Tree looks like for someone who acquires one of the most in-demand skills around these days —**welding**:

ENTRY-LEVEL CAREERS

- Trailer Manufacturing
- Sheet Metal Manufacturer, Welder

- Shop Welding and Repair
- Equipment Welding and Repair

- Fencing Welder
- Aluminum Railing Welder
- Welder's Helper
- Shop Welder, Machinist

- Specialty Parts Manufacturing
- Stainless Steel TIG Welder
- Parts Welder, Assembler
- Cutter, Solderer, Brazer (Ships)

TECHNICAL CAREERS

- Custom Motorsports Fabricator
- Structural Welder
- On-Board Ship Maintenance
- Pipe Fitter
- MIG/TIG Boat Welder
- Project Manager (Foreman)

- Renewable Energy Installation Welder
- Welding Instructor
- Welding Technician
- Welding Sales Rep
- Cutting Specialist (Demolition Crew)
- Welding Machine Operator

PROFESSIONAL CAREERS

- Underwater Welder
- Dry Underwater Welder
- Robotic Welding Specialist
- Weld Inspector
- Material/Weld Engineer
- Weld Engineer

- Military Support Welder
- Industrial Shutdowns
- Oil Rig Welder
- Fabrication Shop Owner
- Pipeline Welder
- Aircraft Welder

These are all real examples of Career Trees used in classrooms, programs, and business training facilities—built by instructors for their unique programs and local labor markets to tell the narrative they wanted to share. But every career field imaginable could have a corresponding Career Tree. And of course, the career branches listed on the wall graphic are just the tip of the iceberg, as there is simply not enough room to show the hundreds of specialized professions and pursuits within each level of each career field. The possibilities are truly endless.

Here's a question for you: did you even know about all the potential career paths out there in these fields? I can admit that I didn't until we began working with teachers to do the research! How can we expect our young people to understand what they want, and how they can get there, if we don't help them connect the dots? How would we think their parents can guide them to the right choice when they don't have all the information either?

One of the most powerful results of the Career Tree is the ongoing conversations it can generate between students and their parents about the kinds of careers they want to pursue. One example comes from Paul Galbenski's school, where he had a student who was extremely interested in becoming a welder and fabricator. (For what it's worth, there is a crisis-level shortage of welders across the country these days.) He also wasn't sure he wanted to go to college.

The challenge in the case of this student was that his father, an engineer by profession, wanted his son to follow in his same career path—which definitely included going to college after graduating from high school. Why? Because that was the career path the father knew best. "I'd say 95 percent of all households know careers related to what people in the family do, but they don't know much about anything else," says Paul.

The fact that the son wanted to pursue a different path caused friction at home. But once the parent came to a Career Night program at the school and had a chance to see the program's Career Tree and all the possibilities open to his son, he softened his stance. Eventually, he and his son reached a compromise where everyone had their needs met: the son enrolled in a university where he is now pursuing a dual degree in engineering and welding and fabrication.

"The real power of the Career Tree is that it helps students find their passion," says Paul. "But it's also a tool that helps teach parents who don't understand that a technical education can be more viable for their child than a four-year degree. It's not an either-or scenario. It's just that you don't have to get a four-year degree to have an outstanding lifestyle and career."[1]

The high school Trees discussed thus far are just one species in a forest of Career Trees that have grown around the needs of many different educational and workforce development environments. These Career Trees encompass middle schools, community colleges, adult learners, special needs students, and corporate settings. In middle schools, the Tree raises awareness of the academic and career programs available for students to explore when they reach high school. At the college level, the Career Tree provides the missing piece of intentional career planning for every student, along with the continuing motivation to persevere to graduation—and beyond. Adult learners, who often return to school amid many other family, work, and life obligations, appreciate how the Career Tree keeps their career goal clearly in view. The special needs Tree doesn't show levels or careers, but rather life skills like "Speaking Up for Myself" and "Asking for What I Need" to help students on their way to the top of the Tree, "Independent Living." In the corporate world, a Tree showing the branch system of company positions inspires current employees to grow their skills and climb to the next level. As a goal-setting exercise and motivational tool, the Career Tree is uniquely effective across a broad range of learning environments.

Creating Pathways to Success

In earlier chapters, I've shared the many traits that make the Why Generation different from the generations that came before. They love the energy of group interactions—which is ideal for the ongoing Career Tree conversations happening in classrooms every day around the country. They have an entrepreneurial bent (especially the younger members of this generational cohort), and the Tree gives them the tools to begin plotting a future based on their independent spirit. They don't want to be merely told that such-and-such career field would be a good fit for them; true to their name of the Why Generation, they want to understand the detailed reasons that their areas of possible career interest will play to their strengths. Reared on social media and the self-disclosure it affords, Why Generation members enjoy the personalized Career Leaf labels that proclaim their career aspirations to their peers and everyone else who views the Tree wall graphic. Finally, as a generation that believes experience is everything, Why Generation members can use the Tree to start planning the experiences and events that will propel them forward in their quest for a rewarding career. It will become the vehicle to connect them with the career experiences they want to have.

How the Light Grows the Tree

Though developed several years before the Career Tree fully bloomed, the Light at the End of the Tunnel motivational strategy ties in perfectly with the Tree's goals and methodology I've described in this chapter. The Career Tree bridges the Awareness Gap for students and parents so that they can discover their own Light at the End of the Tunnel, whatever that motivating desire might be for them. There is no wrong branch or section—everything should be driven by a student's interests, talents, and goals. In many ways the Career Tree is the missing piece of self-discovery, ongoing reflection, and even soul-searching that many students must experience to find their light. By making meaningful, ongoing career exploration the norm rather than the exception, the Career Tree is poised to help close the skills gap by first bridging the Awareness Gap.

The Career Tree also plays a critical role in helping organizations create what I call a *planning culture* that empowers students and employees to figure out their future direction. A planning culture is simply an environment that encourages individuals to set a goal or destination; plan to reach that goal through myriad pathways, opportunities, and research; and continually readjust and calibrate the goal and plan to further hone their purpose and subsequent action.

Empowering young people to take action is the key. A goal and a plan are useless without the will and determination to take the necessary action. The light and "want-to" help to create that will and determination within the individual. Developing a planning culture creates the ongoing, proactive environment necessary for students to see planning as a critical part of a successful life.

One school that has embarked on building a planning culture is Salem-Keizer Public Schools in Salem, Oregon. As Jim Orth, an administrator with the school, puts it: "We are no longer in the college preparation business, but rather in the workforce development business, and it is not too late to accept and act upon this realization."[2]

From Jim's perspective, we are uniquely positioned to assist our students in connecting their interests, skills, and talents to career paths that will empower them to realize their lifestyle desires. By starting career exploration earlier, in middle school or even elementary school, we could engage students in their learning for the purpose of someday finding a career they value as much as the salary required to support the lifestyle they want. By connecting their interests, skills, and talents to academic learning, providing contextual learning within career-focused paths, and emphasizing Professional

Skills, we can propel students toward career readiness—regardless of the education, certification, or experience their chosen career area may require.

The power of a strong planning culture goes far beyond the educational arena and into the world of employment. Earlier I shared a statistic that says 66 percent of younger-generation folks are planning to leave their current job by 2020. If companies are going to find and retain the top talent, a planning culture is critical. In the workplace, a planning culture is an environment where employees plan openly for advancement, opportunities, and growth. This approach takes some of the unspoken guesswork and uncertainty out of the process by keeping communication open and opportunities transparent. Intentional succession planning is another aspect of a planning culture that allows organizations to build from within, before current employees start looking for their next growth opportunity outside the organization. It's not enough anymore to use "stuff" to entice people to stay; they need opportunity, clearly spelled out and ready for the taking if they are motivated enough to take it. People will stay in their current jobs if they are excited about the opportunities ahead of them there. A planning culture is critical for companies to make that happen.

A planning culture also facilitates collaboration and a desire to share your plan with others. When I speak to schools and businesses, I punctuate the importance of fostering a planning culture environment where creating your plan is always accompanied by sharing it with others for their feedback and for accountability. Perhaps part of sharing the plan could even include submitting the plan for public sharing of some kind so it can become an example for others of how to achieve what you want. The sheer power of talking about planning, demonstrating planning, and praising planning raises all ships as the process of planning becomes cool—even sought after. This collaboration and open sharing will create a competitive advantage for the organizations that make it a priority—finding purpose, sharpening focus, increasing performance, and building passion for both individuals and groups.

There's a lot that goes into creating a planning culture, more than I have space to cover in depth here. But really, it starts with realizing the importance of constant goal-setting and recalibration on the way toward that destination. This should be something that every individual associated with the organization takes part in—employees, students, administration, and everyone in between. In my work with teams across the country, creating a planning culture is one of the first and most important things we do. Everyone in the organization can benefit from being intentional about setting goals and planning how to make them happen.

The Career Tree is an effective tool in helping build a planning culture in both the classroom and the workplace, creating new opportunities for Why Generation members to find the branches they want to reach for. Let's help them climb. Once our students or employees set their sights on where they want to go, the next step is helping them create the strong root system to help them reach that destination—which is the subject of our next chapter.

CHAPTER SIX INSIGHTS

- There is a misconception on the part of many people that the younger generations are to blame for being clueless about what they want to do with their lives. But whose fault is that? As parents, educators, and employers, have we truly taught them about the abundance of options available to them?

- We can help young people reach for their goals and climb out on new branches by using tools like the Career Tree to give them insights into the kinds of careers and lifestyles they might be attracted to.

- It's amazing to see young people research careers on their own and then put together a plan for what kinds of education and skills they need to get there.

- There is no right or wrong answer when it comes to selecting a spot on the Career Tree. There's no wrong branch! What the Tree does is help build awareness and interest so that young people can select goals to reach for. Those goals can be shifted higher or lower on the Tree over time as well. It's a dynamic solution that adapts to the desires of the person taking control of their life and educational journey.

- The Career Tree is also a powerful way to show educators and parents that there are many paths young people can take to reach their career goals. College is just one great option among many other equally great choices.

- An organization's planning culture empowers individuals to figure out their future direction by setting a goal or destination, planning to reach that goal, sharing the plan with others, and continually recalibrating that plan. This type of environment is critical not only for success in the classroom but also in the workplace as companies seek to attract and retain the best talent.

- The Career Tree connects perfectly with the Light at the End of the Tunnel by bridging the Awareness Gap so that students know all their options and can truly choose the light that appeals to them.

CHAPTER SEVEN

Building a Competitive Advantage

The intersection of academic knowledge and technical skills is the single most important competitive advantage in today's new economy. And yet, there remains a substantial Awareness Gap, not just among the Why Generation but also among educators and parents. They miss the point that by combining a robust high school education with in-demand technical training, today's students can gain an edge in our increasingly global labor marketplace. But this isn't just high school we're talking about: the same advantages apply to those young people in middle school all the way up to adult learners. Everyone can benefit from the combination of enhanced academic and technical skills. This isn't a surprise to those who work in the field of career and technical education, but it is news to many in our communities and country. And it's news we need to make known.

Meaningful career exploration will bridge the Awareness Gap that has contributed to the skills gap crisis in our country. Young people can only base their career aspirations on what they know, and many have no idea of the vast opportunities in the existing and emerging career fields in the United States today. Students who think they want to go to college for a specific career might change their mind completely after experiencing a career program. Or maybe after experiencing the career program, students will solidify the original decisions made about educational and career direction. The point is, students who take part in career-focused learning have a much wider breadth of knowledge, experience, and guidance from which to make their choices. Career programs are a powerful tool to help them know what they don't know and bridge their personal Awareness Gap.

Not only that, but college-bound students can benefit tremendously from completing a career-focused program in high school. The competitive advantage of career-minded education is not just for students who plan to pursue postsecondary options other than college. Even if the college-bound students' high school career program is not in their career field of choice, they will have gained a lifelong marketable skill that will enable them to earn an above-average wage during their college years, funding their future. Those whose program aligns with their college plans will have a head start on the material, will know with more certainty that this is the right field for them, and will have hands-on experience and networking possibilities that their peers will have to scramble to find. The competitive advantage is evident.

For those planning to attend college, why wait until college to experience your field? Why not start building the foundation that will make your college application more attractive, enable you to earn a higher wage while in college, and give you an edge? And yet too many students not only wait until college to start pursuing their career aspirations, they wait until college to figure out their life and career direction—all while paying for and/or incurring the debt associated with a college education. This is why providing a purposeful education is such a critical philosophy for our success as a nation. Determining a direction in high school allows students to choose, at their discretion, advanced education purposefully, which significantly increases their probability of completing higher education successfully.

Of course, for those who want to pursue a career in their career program field upon high school graduation, career-focused education delivers a clear and immediate competitive advantage. They will graduate with a clearer picture of the industry and what they need to do to reach their desired position. They'll have the skills to enter their profession and build upon that knowledge with additional training and on-the-job learning. Their program sets them up to succeed—and their choices are still wide open. They can change their mind at any time, and the technical and Professional Skills they have gained will go with them wherever their unique pathway leads.

When it comes to career exploration, timing is far more important than many might think. Many adult learners who return to school to obtain a certification or degree for a particular career can attest to the remarkable competitive advantage when a student can discover his or her interest earlier in the educational journey. This was the case for my son Nick. He discovered that he wanted to become a software engineer while he still had time to positively impact his high school performance and lay the foundation to reach that goal. Had he remained unaware of the opportunities in programming and software development, Nick may have scarcely made it out of high school and would possibly be employed today in an unskilled position at a minimal wage. Thankfully, the reverse is true, as he is gainfully employed in the career field he chose in high school and is living a rewarding lifestyle that has led to both self-reliance and independence. We need to make his story far more common than it currently is.

Nick faced a challenge the day he came home and announced his desire to become a software engineer—and it was a major challenge, as he had squandered many days of school, wasn't engaged in his education prior to that day of realization, and was sporting an uninspiring 1.5 cumulative GPA through his sophomore year of high school. Branch creak! He was now in a position where he wanted something, so that deep-seated fear of loss and sense of urgency kicked in and made him uncomfortable. He felt it that night; he knew he had to turn things around, he had to increase his performance, and it was time to get serious about accomplishing something transformative in his life. It was a beautiful day!

The Relevance of Roots

The key strategy behind the Career Tree is to open and maintain the dialogue with adult, high school, and middle school students about the virtues of all branches and sections of the Tree without pushing them toward any one area or branch. All areas are possible and viable. Unlike today's societal pressure for all students to attend college, the Career Tree pushes no preconceived notion or direction—it's based on each student's desires, and every option is on the table. As part of the exploration process, students choose the branch that speaks to them, research the specific career and lifestyle on that branch, and in due course determine the appropriateness of the fit and long-range plan to achieve that goal. But there's far more to the Tree than just the trunk and branches. The majestic spreads of branches and leaves we see would not be possible without something that lies beneath the surface of the ground: the Root System.

If we were looking at Nick's programming and software development Career Tree, software engineer would certainly be in the

Professional Careers section at the top of the Tree since a master's degree in software engineering is required to unlock that branch. Suddenly, Nick needed to attend college and graduate with a degree in computer science. He realized he didn't have the necessary Root System in place to ascend the Tree to his desired branch; after all, he had only a 1.5 GPA. He needed to develop a stronger Root System.

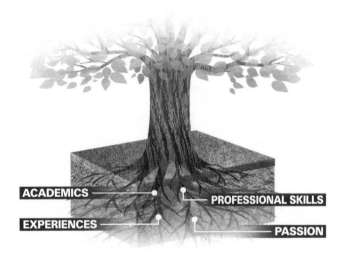

The Career Tree Root System is made up of four critical Roots that provide the foundation for everything else:

Academics. A strong academic background is important to the vast majority of attractive and viable careers in the United States. This realization forced Nick to focus on elevating his GPA and performing better academically. The Tree's Root System brought home the vital relevance of a resilient academic performance for Nick to achieve his desired goal of becoming a software engineer. In many schools across the nation a large number of students are failing academically not because they aren't intelligent, but because they simply do not see the relevance of academic performance. They're the Why Generation, but they have never been shown why academic knowledge is needed in their lives. The younger generations must know why they are accomplishing something; relevance is the key missing factor for increasing performance. The Root System delivers that relevance, as Nick immediately saw how academics now fit into his goal. This is why helping students start with the end in mind always supports their efforts and builds significance for their choices.

Professional Skills. These are the skills required to become a truly career-ready and productive member of the community. As a partial list, they include communication, confidence, decision making, enthusiasm, flexibility, interviewing, leadership, listening, negotiating, networking, presenting, time management, and a positive work ethic. Nick needed to begin developing his Professional Skills so he could ascend the Tree to his desired branch. As part of my keynote speeches, I present the value of changing the term *soft skills* to the term *Professional Skills*, as I believe the first term sounds insignificant and is too often ignored when people look at their education choices in America. Those programs and pathways of study that are coaching full-bodied Professional Skills are preparing adult and high school learners not only for great careers, but also for successful lives.

Professional Skills are so critical to students' future success that one Career Tree organization used the Root System's Professional Skills section to build a database that rates students' specific skills using scoring standards based on input from local business advisory members. This quarterly report motivates students to think about the abilities that aren't always on the job description—attendance, behavior incidents, timeliness, ability to work with others, and more. Seeing a grade for these types of behaviors gives them a weight that they may not otherwise have, thus increasing students' performance in these areas. In addition, students voluntarily submit to random drug testing, and their results appear on their Professional Skills Score report to demonstrate to future employers and college admission officers their commitment to a drug-free lifestyle. The Professional Skills Score is just one example of how innovative teachers and administrators are taking these concepts to the next level. The applications of this concept are truly limitless as more and more educators bring their creativity to bear on the challenges the Why Generation faces.

Is there a parent alive that does not want his or her son or daughter to learn these kinds of Professional Skills? What parents do not want their student to learn leadership, communication, punctuality, and work ethic? For all we extol a college education, why are we not as outwardly passionate about those skills, especially since they create the kind of competitive advantage we want our children to have no matter what their career choice?

Experiences. As the skills gap expands, relevant work and volunteer experience has become the new focus of hiring managers in the candidates they hope to employ. Young people who can demonstrate that they have valuable experiences under their belt have an indisputable edge over those with less robust résumés. And it's never too early to start amassing those irreplaceable experiences and activities—not just for how great they look on a résumé, but for the innate self-discovery and career exploration they deliver.

My father once shared a key piece of advice with me: "It takes focus, planning, and action to assemble the things you accomplish in your life into something meaningful. The things you achieve must stack and support each other in growth toward the outcome that you desire for your life." For Nick, the Root related to Experiences meant that everything he accomplished—such as increasing his academic performance, completing his programming and software development program, participating in internships, working summer jobs, doing consulting projects, and experimenting with projects on his computer every weekend—now added to his experience and résumé. This would make him a more desirable prospective student, employee, and team member. Suddenly he saw the value of pursuing relevant experiences, and he was all in.

Passion. This Root is critical to any endeavor or goal. When the going gets tough, the tough use passion to power through the obstacles that attempt to knock us off course. Passion gives us the vital energy, commitment, enthusiasm, mental focus, and sturdy resolve to overcome the branch creaks that inevitably come throughout long-term goal achievement. Nick would need every bit of passion he could muster to overcome the challenges he faced in the balance of his high school experience, as well as those he would face in college and beyond. His seemingly boundless enthusiasm for accomplishing his objective made him resolute in its long-term attainment.

It's worth noting that passion is not something we as educators, parents, or employers can confer upon the Why Generation no matter how hard we try. Passion has to come from within the young person, born of personal desire and aspirations. Passion also comes from knowing where you are going and why you are going there, building the confidence of doing it successfully, learning what it takes to succeed, and then heading in the right direction. The resulting passion creates confidence and the resolve and determination to see their plan through over the long run.

This is another reason why the self-determined framework of

the Career Tree is so important: the students themselves determine where they want to go in their educational journey and life direction. Secondhand enthusiasm will not see you through when the challenges that are part of your chosen path rise up to stop you. We cannot choose our young people's paths for them, but we can give them the tools and knowledge to make the choice that's right for them and thus generate the passion to persevere.

Growing Opportunities

In essence, like an organic self-sustaining environment, the Root System delivers relevance to the branch system, and the branch system delivers relevance to the Root System. In a symbiotic, circle-of-life, dependent relationship, both the branch and Root Systems work as a continuous reminder of the connection between goals and the skill development required to achieve those intentions.

For too long, we've battled the idea that students who participate in a career program during their high school years have limited their future options and opportunities by doing so. While the "voc-ed" of the past may have focused on equipping workers for very specific jobs, modern career-focused training combines technical-skill attainment with academically rigorous coursework to raise, not lower, the standard of achievement and the range of possibilities. I believe it's time to change the narrative and tell that story. But how?

Today's students will be entering a global economy and workforce that is changing more rapidly than ever. Technology is advancing at an unprecedented pace and will continue to affect every aspect of our lives, careers, economy, and workforce. We owe it to the next generation to help them launch their future with a real edge in college and career. Together, we must champion the cause of making young people career ready not for our own benefit, but for the students whose future success is entrusted to us. It couldn't be in better hands as we share with them this simple message: a career-ready focus expands your options and opportunities for a dynamic competitive advantage in today's new economy.

Let's pick an example: the list of Professional Careers in the Career Tree for an automotive program. I notice that it is possible to unlock either automotive engineer or automotive designer with a four-year degree or beyond. I often ask automotive teachers whether it is possible to take the program in high school, become ASE certified, and then attend college and one day become an automotive engineer or automotive designer. They always answer a definite "Yes." I then ask whether it is possible for a student to avoid the automotive program altogether, finish their academic requirements for graduation, head off to college, and one day become an automotive engineer or automotive designer. Once again, the answer is a definite "Yes." So I ask my audiences all over the world, what is the benefit of students taking the program in high school versus waiting until college to select their course of action? The audiences always erupt in extolling the virtues of taking and completing the high school program instead of waiting to figure it out once the college financial clock has started ticking. A partial list of the many benefits mentioned by my audience members include:

- The students already know whether they like cars enough to pursue the automotive field as a viable career option before spending money to learn if it is a good fit.

- They already have the requisite hands-on, real-world experience needed to become a successful automotive engineer or automotive designer.

- They already know the inner working of cars, how they function, and what it takes to overcome design deficiencies and flaws.

- The students (and parents) will save money by investing wisely in the next level of education—in the end, they will invest in purposeful education.

- The students become ASE certified upon program completion and can earn a higher wage to work their way through higher education, developing the needed experience and income to lower the college debt burden and fund that advanced study.

- The students, by virtue of being ASE certified and gaining the necessary on-the-job experience sooner (which of course comes with working in the field), can become lead candidates for a specialized college course of study, paid internships, and other opportunities available to motivated and successful students. These students, in essence, become the right students, in the right college programs, for the right reasons, with a powerful competitive advantage to achieve more than the students simply starting from square one at some point in the college experience.

Parents, educators, do these sound like truly valuable benefits to you? Do you see what we've done here? We've reframed a program that many people might dismiss as the engine that can not only propel a student through high school but also college and beyond. Rather than putting a student on the path to becoming a grease monkey, now he or she has begun the path to becoming an automotive engineer. And this is only an automotive career example. These same powerful competitive advantages play out in countless fields in every career cluster nationwide, such as:

- Agriculture and Natural Resources
- Architecture and Construction
- Arts, Audio Visual Technology, and Communications
- Business Management and Administration
- Education and Training
- Finance
- Government and Public Administration
- Health Science
- Hospitality and Tourism
- Human Services
- Information Technology
- Law, Public Safety, Corrections, and Security
- Manufacturing
- Marketing
- Science, Technology, Engineering, and Mathematics
- Transportation, Distribution, and Logistics

The value of the high school automotive program can become enormous for the students who want to achieve any level within the Career Tree for that field. It does not matter what branch they choose or how often they modify their choice—it is about their direction and interests, which are at the heart of self-motivation. Each student who performs well in the program achieves a competitive advantage regardless of the section or branch of the Tree chosen. The ongoing dialogue allows teachers and parents to walk students from not knowing what they don't know to knowing what they know and acting on that insight.

The Career Tree also serves as a powerful tool in creating dialogue between teachers and students that can help overcome performance issues. If a student is consistently late for class, for example, the teacher can bring the student over to the Career Tree and point to the leaf that represents the career that student has chosen. "Do you still see yourself rising to this level of the Career Tree?" the teacher can ask. If the student says yes, then the teacher can say: "Great, but if you want to reach it, the Professional Skills at that level dictate that you consistently show up on time. If you don't, you are at risk of falling short of your goal." Rather than punish the student for being late, the teacher can reframe the issue in a way that gives the student the power to change her behavior because she wants to. The Career Tree can help connect the dots for the student in a way that he or she can choose to earn a competitive advantage. Imagine the results of that ongoing student dialogue and insight being used to transform the middle and high school experience for students nationwide.

What would happen to our country's Awareness Gap if the Why Generation was receiving the full range of information about the many exciting options and opportunities out there? The Career Tree is one tool that empowers us to bridge the Awareness Gap by moving students from seeing only one recommended pathway (pursuing a college education) to all pathways and options available based on their unique interests, talents, and abilities. This is useful for students at all ages and levels: middle school, high school, and postsecondary. Each career branch of the Tree has a corresponding lifestyle. The lifestyle associated with each branch plays a huge part of all Why Generation decisions, which is why they must research the career, income, responsibilities, and lifestyle that come with that career choice. Whether students choose college, certification, licensure, apprenticeship, work-based training programs, or other options, they are selecting the pathway that's right for them based on their Light at the End of the Tunnel, the goal of the career they become passionate to attain.

Rethinking What's Possible

I work closely with many amazing educational organizations that have fully embraced the Career Tree strategy. One of these partners built a robust Career Tree that shows an inspiring and powerful pathway through advanced manufacturing. I've mentioned earlier how today, precision machinists are in huge demand because manufacturers can't find young people to fill these skilled positions. It's a high-wage, high-demand field and yet, due to the widening of the skills gap, there's no one qualified to take the job and run with it. Far from the old stereotype of a dead-end factory job, the work now available in this field is so challenging and specialized that it requires a high-caliber individual with nationally certified skills to perform it. Manufacturing today is a whole new world, and public perception hasn't kept up with the reality. Here are just a few of the exciting career branches, selected by instructors in classrooms around the country, that populate this Tree:

ENTRY-LEVEL CAREERS

- Machine Operator
- CNC Operator
- Robot Operator
- Material Handler
- Assembler
- Packager
- Press Operator
- Quality Assistant
- Apprentice
- Stock Cutter/Handler
- Inspector
- Manual Machine Tool Operator

TECHNICAL CAREERS

- Machinist
- Maintenance Machinist
- Millwright
- Quality Control Inspector
- Mold Maker
- Pattern Maker

- Tool and Die Maker
- Instrument Maker
- CNC Programmer
- CNC Machinist
- Machine Builder
- Robot Programmer

PROFESSIONAL CAREERS

- Manufacturing Engineer
- Quality Manager
- Aerospace Manufacturing Manager
- Medical Device Manufacturing Engineer
- Computer Automated Manufacturing Engineer

- Manufacturing Sales Engineer
- Aeronautical Engineer
- Aerospace Engineer
- Metallurgist
- Instructor
- Quality Engineer
- Plant Engineer

It's time to expand the view of what's possible. Our struggling manufacturing sector can explode if we can effectively showcase to the Why Generation the dynamic opportunities and potential of this field. It's not just operating a machine—gaining skills in this field can be a pathway to so many incredible careers, all based on the amount of education someone wants to pursue. Pursuing a career in manufacturing may also lower debt, as workers can make awesome money while moving to their ideal branch on the Tree. (Many manufacturers will also pay employees to pursue higher education!) The amazing opportunities in manufacturing are only one striking example of how we can change the paradigm by expanding the view of what's possible while creating the competitive advantage that comes with early career exploration.

Connecting the Dots

Exceptional performance can happen when students (at any age) engaged in any program, pathway, or course of study take it upon themselves to dive deeply into the Root System to determine how to get where they want to go. Now that they know where they are going, they have to know how they are getting there by creating the plan to get there. This process can happen quickly or over a long period of time. But every step students take in executing their plan locks them in further or shows them why they may need to tweak the plan or their destination. A student might determine the need to add more academic performance, for example, if he or she wants to climb to a higher branch on the Career Tree. It's all part of building a strong planning culture where goal-setting is the norm for every student.

So how does one go about making such a plan? One way would be to begin by asking and answering some questions that will help students create their own plan for reaching their destination. Here are some examples:

ACADEMICS

- What academic subjects will you need to focus on to reach your career goal?

- What level of education or training is required to reach your chosen career? (industry certification, degree, license, and so on)

- How much will your postsecondary education cost?

EXPERIENCES

- What experiences will help you discover more about your chosen career? (part-time jobs, volunteering, on-site job visits, and so on)

- If your field offers volunteer, internship, or
  apprenticeship opportunities, where would you
  like to experience this?

PROFESSIONAL SKILLS

- What Professional Skills do you feel you
  already possess?

- What types of Professional Skills are most important
  in your chosen career?

- Are there any Professional Skills you will need
  to grow?

PASSION

- What is exciting to you about your chosen career?

- What kind of lifestyle will your chosen career help
  you to enjoy?

- How will you re-motivate yourself when your goal
  seems distant or difficult?

The power of this approach is that the student is the one doing the research to answer these questions. It connects their "want-to" with the "how-to." They embark on a journey of discovery that will ultimately lead them to the Light at the End of the Tunnel.

Another educational partner of mine is a motivated technical high school team that is using the Career Tree with great success. Their state has developed a dynamic and effective four-year regional technical high school system where each technical high school has a full range of career and technical education programs coupled with robust academics, sports, cheerleading, and more. I work with numerous high-achieving schools in the state, but the 14 professionals on this particular team all stand out as being passionate about making a difference in students' lives.

The teacher of the electrical program was describing his use of the Career Tree and the impact it made on his current students as well as prospective new students and their parents who had attended an open house several weeks earlier. He said that the impact of the Tree had not only changed the dynamic in his classroom, but also his entire perception of his own career.

In partnership with my team at TFS, he developed a hearty Tree with abundant branches in all sections representing the most viable, relevant, and living-wage types of careers and occupations possible as a result of completing his electrical program. Using our TFS Career Tree Curriculum Guide and wall-mounted Career Tree visual, he asked his class to pick something on the Tree. Each student picked things that seemed interesting and began the research necessary to understand the career and lifestyle associated with each position. One of those branches was that of a career called marine electrician, which intrigued several students.

As he continued to share this story with the team I was working with that day, the teacher asked, "What do you suppose a marine electrician does?" We all looked around at each other and took some wild guesses. One person said it was the electrician who works underwater in scuba attire and fixes underwater cabling. Another guessed that it was an electrician working for the marines. And yet another guessed that it was someone who worked with electricity in a marina. Turns out we were all wrong.

One of his students, let's call her Mary, was so fascinated that she chose the marine electrician career to research in depth, including the career itself, daily responsibilities, salary range, work schedule, and lifestyle. What came out of Mary's research was remarkably eye opening. She learned that a marine electrician is the person who works as an electrician on a cruise ship such as Royal Caribbean,

Carnival, and Silver Sea. These types of floating cities need teams of electricians, carpenters, and maintenance professionals to keep things operating at peak efficiency while at sea.

Mary also learned that this kind of position pays $65,000 to $75,000 per year, and the employee lives on the ship, traveling everywhere the paying customers do, but at little to no cost. Mary thought that was infinitely cool and also realized that meant you would have virtually no living expenses. When Mary explained to her classmates everything she had learned about what it meant to be a marine electrician, five of them raised their hands and said: "I want to do that!" Mary and several others became extremely excited at the prospect of working as marine electricians and seeing the world via that career choice. That moment became their perfect intersection of career and lifestyle. It's worth emphasizing that a significant factor in every decision a member of the Why Generation makes is an assessment of how it will impact lifestyle. It's powerful to see young people make that connection between where they want to be and why, which then becomes the fuel, the Light at the End of the Tunnel, to power and guide them to reach their destination.

Mary and her fellow students used Career Leaf labels to write their names and career choice and placed them on the Tree, making marine electrician their goal and Light at the End of the Tunnel. Those students became excited and focused, started planning, and were now ready to take action based on their newfound knowledge and passion.

The teacher went on to explain the huge "aha" moment for him. Ever since he started teaching many years ago, almost every Why Generation student who took his program had always thought that an electrician is simply that person who comes to your house and puts up a fixture or rewires an outlet. That all changed as he started sharing the true possibilities of this field with his high school students and expanding their knowledge of the many potential careers and occupations that are possible as a result of completing his program.

He added that even the new parents who had come to the open house several weeks prior to my visit were excited about the expanded opportunities and options available to their son and daughters. Parents stood in front of the Career Tree on his wall, asked questions, and probed to fully understand the power of this simple visual display and goal-setting tool. It significantly increased their knowledge of how robust academics and strong technical skills can create a powerful competitive advantage for their children, regardless of whether they were going to college, launching a career, or doing whatever they desired as a next step after high school. It opened up the playing field and created a wide range of possibilities. It helped to close the Awareness Gap they didn't even know they had.

Finally, he explained that using the Tree made him a better teacher, as it allowed him to know where all of his students saw themselves in the future. He could then plan more relevant field trips, guest speakers, and examples each day. It also allowed him to bring tremendous relevance to students' academic performance as part of their Root System, as that was now all connected to their long-term success.

This is just one of a remarkable number of stories that have come out of helping students and trainees make the transition from not knowing what they don't know to knowing what they know and acting on that knowledge. "It's so powerful when you see students sitting down and using the Career Tree to map out the lifestyle they want and the money they want to make," says Cathie Raymond. "It's such a powerful visual giving them the chance to place that leaf on a branch or to even move it around. It just helps to give them so much focus in where they want to go."

The outcome for middle school, high school, community and technical college, and university students as well as workforce development trainees can be significantly increased with the exploration, discovery, and development of the goal (destination), keeping that goal firmly in view, and working to develop the corresponding Root System, knowledge, and skills to thrive.

In today's changing landscape of education and workforce development, we face huge challenges such as the expanding skills gap in America, the inability of many businesses to find a motivated and empowered workforce that takes personal ownership, rising college costs, and lagging student performance at almost every level of education. The branch is creaking, and it is time to truly inspire Why Generation members by capturing their hearts and minds with the insight of a great many options and opportunities available to them based on their own unique interests, talents, and abilities. It is time to make students more than "college and career ready"—we need to make them "career ready," period.

This is a self-motivated path that leads to self-reliance and independence, as in the case of my son Nick and the countless students who are positively impacted each year by the motivating teachers who inspire, coach, and mentor students in the direction of their own goals and Light at the End of the Tunnel. If you're an educator, you can truly make a difference when you take the initiative to tell students what they don't know and provide an environment that supports early career exploration. And it all starts with a conversation.

CHAPTER SEVEN INSIGHTS

- Because of the Awareness Gap, young people today simply do not know about the attractive career opportunities in many high-demand fields. Meaningful career exploration can help bridge that gap.

- Whether college, career, or additional postsecondary training is on the immediate horizon, every student can benefit from the combination of enhanced academic and technical skills.

- In order to climb the Career Tree, young people today need a competitive advantage. That's why establishing a strong Root System of skills and traits is so critical to the success of any young person.

- The Root System of the Career Tree can become a dynamic plan of study to help students get where they want to go, faster.

- An early focus on making young people career ready builds the kind of competitive advantage that helps breed success over the long run.

- With employers demanding more skilled workers, embracing career readiness training and learning Professional Skills, such as the ability to communicate effectively, can be game-changers for young people as they enter the workforce.

- Pathways like electricity may seem limited, but in reality they are full of unexpected and attractive options, as Mary discovered in her quest to find out more about the work and lifestyle of marine electricians. Her experience demonstrates the power of having students research careers for themselves based on their own interests and curiosity.

SECTION THREE

Take Action
on the Plan

CHAPTER EIGHT

Education with Purpose; Employment with Passion

"When am I ever going to use this?"

Have you ever heard this question from an unengaged young person? What he or she is really asking is, "What is the value and relevance of this particular subject to my real life? How will I benefit from learning this?" When we answer these questions, we are attempting to contextualize the learning process, to ground it in reality. Contextual learning is a growing trend in education—and in my opinion it can't grow fast enough.

What is contextual learning? One definition states that it "involves making learning meaningful to students by connecting to the real world. It draws upon students' diverse skills, interests, experiences, and cultures and integrates these into what and how students learn and how they are assessed."[1] It is often hands-on. It may be off-site. It seeks to simulate or enter real-world situations to maximize concept and skill attainment and retention. Contextual learning experiences can include internships, apprenticeships, and service learning opportunities. It's education made real and connected to the innate curiosity, talents, and goals of each student.

A quote sometimes attributed to Benjamin Franklin says: "Tell me and I forget. Teach me and I remember. Involve me and I learn." In his famous "Cone of Learning," American educator Edgar Dale claims that over a two-week period we remember only

- 10 percent of what we read,
- 20 percent of what we hear,
- 30 percent of what we see,
- 50 percent of what we hear and see,
- 70 percent of what we say and write, and
- 90 percent of what we actually participate in.[2]

It's clear that the more involved we are with the material, the more we grasp and remember over the long term. Not surprisingly, researchers have found that many people engage more deeply in the learning process—and better remember what they've learned—when they encounter new concepts within their context.[3]

Why is contextual learning so effective? It can motivate otherwise unengaged students, build confidence, spark the enthusiasm to achieve, and direct students to think about and set long-term goals for their education and career journeys. Contextual learning is part of why the Career Tree is motivating students nationwide to perform at a higher level because it shows the relevance of their education to the life and career they want to have.

The best contextual learning is largely self-directed, giving students ownership of the experience and encouraging them to learn not just from the instructor, but also from each other. Career-focused education is one route that offers so many examples of contextual learning, like flying a drone to record video of the extensive property of a residence going on the market, expertly wrapping a sports injury at a football game, programming and calibrating high-tech robots to follow complex commands in the advanced manufacturing arena, or working as part of a precision automotive race team focused on top performance. These are all what are called "authentic tasks," real needs and problems that are being solved by the students in the course of their learning experience.

There are hundreds, maybe thousands, of examples like these taking place without fanfare every day in the career-focused education programs around the country. And it's making a difference. Students are grasping the concepts, graduating in greater numbers, and pursuing purposeful postsecondary training as a result.

The best way to answer the "when am I ever going to use this?" question is to address it before it's even asked. Teachers in every discipline, both technical and academic, should start the first day asking what students love to do and what experiences they want to have and then connect the course or subject to the attainment of those dreams. Take them on field trips. Bring in experts to talk about what the industry is really like. Let them get their hands dirty and their feet wet—and have fun as they do it. If we want to be contextual educators, we must highlight the relevance of the learning topic every day by connecting the dots for our students. When we do this proactively, we set them up to learn more, remember more, and achieve more in the classroom and beyond.

Introducing Education with Purpose®

There are pros and cons for every educational path: college, trade school, vocational or career and technical education, and the seesaw battle of community college versus university. It's an amazing hodgepodge of alternatives, all sporting distinct pros and cons based on what an individual is trying to accomplish. There's one absolute truth, however, that I have learned throughout my journey—and that is that education for education's sake alone can simply become a tremendous waste of time and money. Far too many young people today are heading off to college without a plan because they and their parents are being sold the notion that they are better off getting that diploma, regardless of the field of study. The impression I receive from many students and parents is that a viable and living-wage profession will wonderfully appear at the end of that journey. That is not always the case; in far too many instances today, it is the exception rather than the rule. Something has to change. Kevin Fleming frames this problem perfectly when he says that most of us have been taught to first pick a college to attend, then pick a major, and when we finally graduate, then decide on what job we want to do. But shouldn't we be doing the opposite? Wouldn't it make more sense if we first chose a career we wanted and then chose a program of study at a school that would help us obtain the skills and education we need to thrive in our chosen career?

Many schools realize they need more focused career counseling—but it doesn't always get the priority it deserves. Kevin talks about the school counselors who are overwhelmed on a daily basis with the sheer number of students who need help discovering the best path for their future. Career exploration is not a one-and-done event that can be completed in one appointment. Events like Career Day—just one day a year—are far too insufficient to help students make better, more informed choices.

This need for a change, to create the kind of widespread planning culture that helps connect young people with an action plan for their future, is what led me to create an approach that I call **Education with Purpose**®. If we can transition students earlier in their journeys to knowing what they know and give them the ability to act on that knowledge, then significantly more students will pursue the kind of education they need based on where they want to go in their lives. This is much different from simply trying to figure out life in college with that enormous financial clock ticking. If they start earlier (and I'm talking in the middle school and high school years), they will be pursuing education with purpose and not education simply for education's sake. Whatever they choose to pursue after high school starts first with the end in mind. Setting the goal becomes the catalyst for selecting a direction and pathway that best suits each student based on their unique interests, talents, and abilities.

That's a message that's been embraced by educators across the country like Michelle Martinez, who helped implement Education with Purpose at a career training school in Arizona. "Everything we do here explains the purpose and why," says Michelle. "We are constantly focused on explaining what's in it for the student. It's our job to give relevance to the rigor." When students show up for class at the school, they know they can expect to be taught skills and capabilities that will be useful to them down the road. For example, students interested in a career in law enforcement will visit their local police precinct and jail while also learning how to handcuff someone. But if they change their mind about what they want to do, the educators are there to listen and help them change course. "It's a constant conversation on how to help the students to get where they want to be by giving them the tools and skills they need to get there," says Michelle, who says that even choir teachers can help their students learn communication and presentation skills that will help them in their future endeavors.[4]

Though I call it Education with Purpose, this principle has application in the business world as well because creating a planning culture becomes a competitive advantage not just in attracting students, but top talent as well. Imagine igniting the fire of ambition in your new employees from their first day onward by showing them a clear picture of the amazing opportunities in your company.

With passion, training, and experience, your employees can rise to the challenge of your most demanding and satisfying careers—but you have to show them how. Education with Purpose could also be called **Employment with Passion** because it's all about planting and nurturing a seed early on, whether in an educational or business context. If you're an employer, read this chapter with an eye to your own company's training methodology and objectives—and with the goal of creating pathways for your employees to find the Career Tree branch they want to climb within your organization instead of forcing them to look outside for their next opportunity. I believe this planning culture philosophy can have a powerful impact on the way businesses approach employee development—ultimately enabling you to maximize your productivity and remain competitive in your market by attracting and retaining young people who see a future with your organization.

Helping young people understand what kinds of skills they will eventually need in their careers is a great way to inspire and engage them in the classroom and beyond into the workplace. One of Michelle's former students, who is now enrolled in a university biomedical program on a track to become a pediatrician, was once a struggling student in high school—especially in subjects like science and math. But once she identified her Light at the End of the Tunnel and knew what kind of branch she wanted to reach on the Career Tree, everything clicked for her. She was able to enroll in a class at school that specifically focused on building the skills she would later need and, while she was cautioned that the effort would be challenging, she rose to the occasion. "It gave her an incentive to work hard and do better academically," says Michelle, "and it also helped her understand how much she wanted to pursue that career well before she got to college." As a footnote to this inspiring story, that student happened to graduate as the valedictorian of her senior class. How's that for a turnaround? And all because she discovered the purpose behind her education—and the passion for her employment.

If, like me, you have heard various branch creaks in your life that have forced you to make positive changes, you probably know the desire to help others do the same in their lives. In my capacity as the founder and CEO of TFS, I have heard a great many branches creaking within our current educational and workforce development systems. Based on these observations, I am convinced that we are in the midst of a major crisis in the United States due to the Awareness Gap of the Why Generation and the resulting skills gap. We are not properly preparing nearly enough students to achieve relevant skills for a living-wage career beyond their high school years.

As parents and educators, we are far too focused on simply promoting high school students to the rank of college student as opposed to helping students at a much younger age focus on career possibilities in the full spectrum of opportunities. College is one of many viable pathways to achieve the needed skills to earn an above-average wage in a rewarding field, but it is not the only (nor always the best) option. The examples I will use are my Education with Purpose; Employment with Passion philosophy and my Career Tree strategy, not because they are the only answers, but because I have witnessed firsthand the incredible ways they can positively impact today's young people in the areas of setting personal goals, discovering life direction, and achieving more when their branch creaks.

As I've stated earlier, we cannot merely make students college and career ready. We must strive to make them all career ready, period. Self-reliance and independence must be the goal. Far too many students head off to a university ill prepared for the eventualities of the availability of jobs, the true costs associated with their education, and the debt burden accompanying their investment. According to one study, fully 62 percent of Americans with student loan debt did not attend any financial aid information sessions prior to enrolling in college.[5] Students who graduated in 2016 average a staggering and record $37,000 in student loan debt[6]—but only 20 percent of them feel prepared for their careers.[7] An even lower number of business leaders, just 11 percent, think these college graduates are ready for the real world of work.[8] The lack of career and loan guidance does students a disservice because they are spending time exploring careers in college while the financial clock is ticking. We should be preparing students much earlier with an understanding of the many careers and pathways that are right for them based on their unique interests, talents, and abilities. One size does not fit all, and there are tremendous opportunities that are overlooked every day in this country. Industries such as advanced manufacturing, construction, aviation, and many more are teeming with open high-wage positions, but these industry employers can't find enough motivated and engaged young people who want to work in those occupations, partially because of the stigma we as a nation attach to those positions.

Education with Purpose means that if you are going to go to college, go with purpose, invest wisely, and get it done. Know why you are going, and avoid the pitfalls of treating college itself as the goal. The goal for a student is not simply to go to college; the goal is to finish college and get a job that pays a living wage in a field he or she loves.

The same applies for students who plan to take any other postsecondary education path. I would tell them: go with purpose, invest wisely, get it done, and get going with the career you chose. Keep your light clearly in view and push through the tunnel of your learning experience with perseverance and resilience. Whether college or other postsecondary training is your plan, pursuing your personal Education with Purpose will help you focus your time and energy, avoid unnecessary debt, and enjoy the satisfaction of reaching your goals faster.

I have observed countless students who, rather than meandering through the college experience hoping to find a spark of direction, have pursued their higher education with energy and excitement for what lies ahead. They've experienced Education with Purpose in high school and are focused, eager, and motivated to do the work and reach their dream career. They have a vision of what that career and lifestyle will be like, and they're hungry to achieve it.

That's a message that Paul Galbenski of Oakland County Public Schools embraces wholeheartedly. "Our rallying point with everything we do is focused on the right student in the right program for the right reasons," he says. "Our curriculum design is working backwards from a student's Light at the End of the Tunnel. It's the anchor for everything we do. We want to get them career ready." Paul points to the fact that his school offers one of the few cosmetology programs left in the state. By focusing on the kind of classes and skills they need while they are still in high school, his students can earn the credits and skills necessary to achieve a cosmetology license when they graduate—something that normally takes two years to complete. "From the very first day of school we talk to them about where they want to go," says Paul. "And our job is to help them learn what they need to get them there."[9]

As Paul's organization demonstrates, an intentional focus on Education with Purpose should start from the first moment a student walks into the building. But consider what usually happens during the first 10 days of school. For many educators, it's schedules, syllabi, rules, and regulations as we acclimate ourselves and our students to the new school year. "Housekeeping" items take precedence. But from my years of research on increasing enrollment and retention with the Why Generation, I am convinced that we need to take a different approach. The most important thing we can do during those first 10 days is to show the Light at the End of the Tunnel—all the exciting rewards that students will enjoy once they've finished their program or pathway.

The Why Generation as a rule doesn't make long-term commitments, and the first 10 days of school are our trial period. We have 10 days and one chance to engage their imagination and convince them that our classes are awesome gateways to a desirable lifestyle where they can have amazing experiences at any level, regardless of where they ultimately see their Light at the End of the Tunnel. If we don't grab this opportunity with both hands, our students may decide this is boring and disengage. Or worse, disappear.

And that's why tools like the Light at the End of the Tunnel and the Career Tree are so critical. They motivate. They inspire. And they remind our students why they wanted to do this in the first place. They make a planning culture second nature because the future is always in view and under discussion. Instead of meeting them with requirements and red tape, we should be capturing their imaginations from the very first moment by helping them see, hear, feel, and experience the amazing things that await them when they finish the coursework. If they're going to succeed, they need to get a good look at their personal Light at the End of the Tunnel.

I know an English teacher named Amy who has taken this idea and run with it. Rather than digging right into her lesson plan, she spends her entire first two classes asking her students questions that engage them by making them feel unique, special, and important. Amy is building on lessons learned from folks who used to sell encyclopedias door-to-door (can you imagine how tough that was?) where the salesperson's goal was to simply get the person who answered the door to say yes to a few simple questions as a way of priming his or her mindset. What Amy has done is make the time to get personal with her students.

She might ask for a show of hands to the question: "How many of you like to do fun things after school?" Of course, everyone says yes. "How about going to the movies?" Or, "How many of you like to go on vacation?" Again, everyone in the class says yes.

Once she feels like she has her students primed, she can dig further. "What do you do for fun?" Amy will ask each one of her students. "What kind of movies do you like?" Again, she engages every student as a way to get them to relax and participate. And she keeps going, asking other questions like: "Who's your favorite band?" "Ever get to see them live?" "If you could travel anywhere in the world, where would you go?" And more. The class responds eagerly to the sense of fun and connection, not only with their teacher but also with each other. Amy's strategy is helping kids recognize the shared connections they might not have known about otherwise (while also probably thinking that this is the best class ever). Not only has she made each student feel unique, special, and important, she has also established a deep level of mutual respect.

Little do they know that their teacher has bigger plans in mind.

The next day, after more discussion about the things they enjoy, she suddenly zeroes in on the point. She asks the class: "So we talked about all these things you love to do. How many of you want to do those same things as an adult?" Every student's hand goes up. "Great," she says. "So how many of you think you need a job to be able to pay for those experiences?" Again, everyone raises their hands. "Perfect," she says. "Now I want you to understand how the things we are learning in this classroom together can help you eventually get the kind of job or jobs that will help you afford all those experiences you want in your life." In her ingenious way, Amy has explained this to her students: if you apply yourself to learning and succeeding in school now, each of you can experience all these great things you love because you will learn the skills you need to get the kind of job to be able to afford the lifestyle you want. Amy makes the idea of studying English both relevant and personal to her students. She answers the question every member of the Why Generation is asking: WIIFM—What's In It For Me? What's in it for me if I work hard to succeed in this class? By uncovering the things they're passionate about, Amy makes them feel valued, all the while connecting the dots between their education and the motivation they need to take it seriously. She shines the Light at the End of the Tunnel—and her students consistently respond with enthusiastic commitment.

This story illustrates Paul Galbenski's point that educators need to be focused on explaining why a student is learning something and how that ties back to their career path. For example, he remembers one young woman, let's call her Becky, who was enrolled in his school's machining program. One day in class, the assignment was to cut out what amounted to a metal comb with a set of teeth set at a certain angle. Becky went to work and produced a halfway-decent product. But when her instructor asked her how she figured out how to set the angles on the teeth of the comb, she admitted she had guessed. Becky's instructor then reminded her of the trigonometry principles she was learning in her math class and how she could have used those formulas to calculate the perfect angles for her comb. "Oh!" Becky said. "Now I get how to use that!" And she went right back to work and created a flawless product once she understood why she was learning what she was learning and its connection to real life. That's powerful stuff and illustrates what can happen when you help paint the complete picture to the members of the Why Generation in your sphere of influence.

There is an opportunity to apply concepts like the Light at the End of the Tunnel and the Career Tree to open up new possibilities and pathways for students that may or may not include heading directly to college after high school.

Consider the story of a young man named Armando from rural Oklahoma. When he was in high school, Armando had the good fortune to enroll in Metro Technology Centers while also taking his regular academic classes. According to Billie Smith, a client of mine who works at Metro Tech and who knows Armando, he was initially a shy kid who came from a large Hispanic family, most of whom held hourly low-wage jobs. Armando had a huge Awareness Gap and college wasn't on the radar at all, as no one from his family had ever gone there.

But Armando got the chance to expand his possibilities by using the Career Tree, where he decided he wanted to become a video game designer. All of a sudden, his education had purpose. At the same time, Armando was introduced to the software design tool AutoCAD® in a technical drafting class he had decided to enroll in. He took to it immediately. Armando was so good at using the software that when a civil engineer came to the school as a guest speaker, Armando's instructor introduced them with an eye on further expanding Armando's career options. As it turns out, the engineer and Armando hit it off, and the engineer offered Armando a paid internship at his engineering firm as a drafting technician where he could put his AutoCAD skills to real use.

Today as a high school graduate, Armando continues to work at the firm, which is also funding the classes he is now taking at the local community college. While Armando could have jumped right into college after graduation, he decided he could learn the skills he needed by working and taking classes part time. Even better, he wouldn't need to take on any debt. His Education with Purpose has led to Employment with Passion as he eyes the next branch on his way up the Tree.

Armando has also reconsidered his place on the Career Tree. First he abandoned the idea of designing video games in favor of becoming an architect. Then he realized his real love: physics. He really likes the science aspect of how buildings come together. So the classes he is taking at the community college are specifically chosen to help him on his path and will be completely transferable if and when he decides to transfer to a four-year college. This is a perfect illustration of what we mean when we say Education with Purpose; Employment with Passion. Armando is one of countless young people, gainfully employed, who are getting educated on what they want to accomplish without wasting time and money on what they don't need.

Our changing landscape of education and workforce development demands that a student possess both academic and technical skills to be successful. There are millions of jobs available but millions of people out of work—and we need to close that skills gap by driving career development into middle schools and high schools to expose students to all the available careers, opportunities, and pathways. Empowering students to select a pathway based on their unique interest is the key to helping them focus, plan, and take the necessary action in the direction of their "want-to," a chosen field based on both the career and lifestyle advantages that appeal directly to each student.

CHAPTER EIGHT INSIGHTS

- Contextual learning answers the question "why?" before it even arises. Once young people have established their Light at the End of the Tunnel and know which branch they want to climb on the Career Tree, contextual learning will keep them engaged.

- Education with Purpose means giving middle school, high school, and postsecondary students the career exploration opportunities, knowledge, and tools to invest wisely and purposefully in the next level of their education. It's a planning culture in action.

- Education with Purpose leads to Employment with Passion, as students who have ascended the Career Tree to their desired branch are motivated to keep climbing when they reach the world of work.

- Employers should also consider how they can build a planning culture that will better create connections and pathways for young people to find the careers they want within their organization.

- Education for education's sake alone can simply become a tremendous waste of time and money, which is why we need philosophies like Education with Purpose to help students invest wisely in their postsecondary learning.

- It's no longer sufficient to teach students the way we always have. We need to answer the why: connecting them with the rationale for learning a subject and how it will help them reach their desired lifestyle and career goals.

- The Light at the End of the Tunnel is the focus of English teacher Amy's first two classes, where she engages students with what they love and then shows them how her subject is relevant to the life they want to enjoy.

- Educators and employers need to rethink their approach to young people with these ideas in mind. How can you better connect with young people and establish a deep level of mutual respect with them?

CHAPTER NINE

Strategies and Tools to Connect and Empower

In this chapter, I offer you the most helpful and universal strategies I and others have developed for understanding and interacting with the Why Generation, whether in the workforce, educational settings, or even your home. These strategies will motivate and empower young people to perform at their full potential and ultimately change the world for the better. No matter where you sit—administrator, teacher, critical support staff member, businessperson, manufacturer—these strategies can be adapted to and be beneficial for nearly every area of work and life. You can adjust them to where you are and the exact audience you serve.

Lots of Challenges

The young people of the Why Generation want lots of challenges, although they require a clear road map and the resources necessary to complete each goal. They find it difficult to be given a long-range goal without the corresponding steps needed to achieve that goal. Breaking down goals into steps and offering the information and resources necessary to meet challenges head-on is important.

In addition, a clear vision of the Light at the End of the Tunnel is vital. It can't be said enough: they also need to understand the big picture of why they are doing what is being asked of them. The big picture is that 10,000-foot view of how this goal or objective is impactful, meaningful, and worthwhile enough to invest time, energy, and their unique, special, and important skills and resources.

Supportive Education and Work Environment

The Why Generation requires and demands a supportive environment, but the support has to come from two directions. They need active and firm support from both their superiors and their peers. If one of those groups is out of sync or incongruent, you stand the chance of disengaging them. Never underestimate the power of social interaction and connection—it can be paramount to their ability to achieve long-term success and acceptance.

Having a supportive education and work environment may seem to be an obvious recipe for success, but we do need to define what support means to the Why Generation. What a baby boomer might consider a supportive work environment is not necessarily how a Why Generation member would view it, so it's important to approach this particular strategy in tandem with the many other insights shared in this book. I view the creation of a supportive education and work environment not as a strategy that is separate and distinct from the others, but as a culmination and combination of them all. The many strategies discussed in this chapter in particular must all be viewed as working together to inspire, empower, and connect with young people. In other words, it's not just one thing, it's lots of things that make the real difference.

Formal Structure

Many elements in the lives of Why Generation members have been structured and orchestrated to achieve the best experience possible, so structure is extremely helpful when they move into the arena of education and ultimately the workforce. When they establish that Light at the End of the Tunnel for themselves, they want to know how they can achieve at a higher level. Clearly delineated steps in the ladder of success are critical to today's young people. They want to know and understand the curbs, what they can and can't do, and how to do it most effectively. This is why "here are tips for success" is a much more productive approach than "these are the rules." Positioning advice and direction through the positive lens of tips for success creates a buy-in and respect for what it truly takes to be successful.

Interactive Relationships

The Why Generation thrives on the steady use of technology to remain remarkably connected and informed. And yet in many school and workplace environments, these same devices that have allowed us to connect to information 24 hours a day, seven days a week are treated as taboo for fear that they will be a significant distraction. In many cases the opposite is true; when used properly and within proper (and communicated) etiquette, technology can be a tremendous advantage that should be harnessed.

Ultimately, young people want to stay connected, use technology, and communicate through social media in order to research, crowd-source, and solve real-world challenges. They want their interactive relationships to be both interpersonal and electronic.

Their biggest challenges come in the use of that technology and the understanding that what they post, text, and blog about online exists forever. It becomes part of their identity. Additionally, since we now live in a world that communicates in 280 characters or less, our English language usage has been reduced to brief message fragments that cut to the point, albeit at times the acronyms can be mystifying. FWIW (or for the benefit of my generation, "for what it's worth"), these abrupt fragments of communication are quite different from the way I routinely correspond, and it has taken some getting used to as a baby boomer.

For instance, I write a text message like I write a letter: it has a beginning, a middle, and an end. This isn't always the norm today. Have we grown too abrupt and in some cases cryptic as feelings, courtesies, and even some meaning are exchanged for brevity that can sometimes feel harsh? Trust me, I believe in short and sweet. But we have become so brief that often the reader wonders, "What did he mean by that?" In an attempt to soften the message and add the emotion back, we use a flood of available emojis that seem to counterbalance some of the bluntness. But ultimately it seems like short, impersonal pieces of communication are flying across our smartphone screens, and fewer people have the time to enjoy real, heartfelt exchanges.

To illustrate that point, I will write a text to my son Nick that includes a salutation, the body of information I want to impart or action I am requesting he take, and the closing in which I write something personal and heartfelt like "Have a great day, love, Dad." After writing a well-thought-out, several-times-reviewed-and-tweaked text, I hit Send . . . only to receive back a short one-letter response several hours later. You guessed it: "k."

I find this humorous, as I run a business and am constantly traveling throughout North America delivering keynote addresses while consulting with many unique organizations—and my son only has time to type one character several hours later. He is apparently so busy that he doesn't even have time to add the "o" in front of the "k." Is that really how far we have come? What frequently confounds me is that he spends much of his time on his phone texting other people, so how could he possibly take several hours to send a one-letter reply to me? We send millions of texts a day, we are more connected than ever, and yet it seems like our intimate interpersonal exchanges have been reduced down to their lowest common denominator . . . a single letter.

While it's easy to bemoan the bare minimum that communication has often become, it is not really the tragedy some would claim. There will always be distinct differences in the way that I write a message and how my sons communicate, and that's okay. They don't have to be me, and my way is not the only right one. The key when engaging members of the Why Generation is to understand that their brevity does not necessarily mean lack of interest or disrespect. It is simply the way they have been wired to respond in a world where short, snippet-like statements on social media and Twitter's 280-character limit are the norm.

Social media, of course, has changed everything. Today anyone can tweet a thought to their followers and ultimately reach a worldwide audience if it is passed along through enough members, even faster if it becomes a trending topic. Social media has become a game changer for individuals and businesses, as it gives anyone a platform to say anything, to anyone, and that message does not have to be positive.

In fact, prior to the social media explosion, companies and individuals could skate past a bad review, negative experience, or just someone who became unhappy with them for whatever reason. Not so easy today . . . you have to deal with the incident, but you also have to consider how those individuals post on their own social media feeds, blogs, and feedback channels moving forward. That negative review, comment, or feedback can live on the Internet for an impressively long time. As a result, many companies now hire teams of social-media-savvy young people to monitor the web and social media outlets in order to respond immediately to those who have a complaint.

Awhile back, I had a less-than-enjoyable experience at United Airlines, where I fly almost all of my 180,000 miles per year. After making a harmless, funny comment on Twitter about my experience that day, I was pleased to receive an almost-immediate response from the team at United asking if there was anything they could do to help. Candidly, there was nothing they could do at that point, but it was refreshing to have them reach out and at least ask if something was possible. I felt better, and that helped ensure that I would not go back online to post any additional negative comments.

Why Generation members thrive on these abundant sources of media as they maintain that needed connection to one another, but they can also use that same technology to become more productive and connected to vast repositories of information that are literally accessible at their fingertips.

Giving them the freedom, tools, and etiquette to use their own technology effectively is a game-changer that delivers a powerful competitive advantage. Starting tech integration at an early age, continuing it in school classrooms, and eventually carrying capabilities to workplace environments will support increased performance in a vigorous competitive global economy. This technology integration pays off for the student and employee, but ultimately pays off significantly for the school and employer.

High Expectations

As I travel North America helping educators and businesses understand the Why Generation, it amazes me that when I arrive at the bullet point in my speech that addresses high expectations, I occasionally hear sighs from several participants. I launch into framing my point and explain that young people have high expectations of everything in their lives except . . . and I pause to see what the audience will add . . . and almost always they add "themselves." Yes, in many cases it seems that the young people of the Why Generation have extremely high expectations of everything in their lives except themselves.

This seems odd to me because we have tried so hard as a generation to help young people develop high self-esteem, and the opposite seems to have occurred. Self-esteem, self-worth, and self-respect would intuitively lead to someone championing higher expectations, but far too many young people today do not connect with high personal expectations or see themselves through the lens of high expectations.

I have found this to be true except for the members of the Why Generation who have a clearly defined Light at the End of the Tunnel and a vision of how they will reach that light. Their Awareness Gap is bridged and they are moving purposefully through their education and career journey. Circling back to earlier thoughts, if the "want-to" is strong enough, the "how-to" will come. Many factors contribute to high self-esteem, but a shared vision can be an important foundation among those elements.

Young people want to believe, they want to belong, they want to give back, and yes, they want to meet high performance expectations. I can't say it enough: they are an incredible generation. They just need to see the light, buy into their own vision, and share in their organization's mission of accomplishing something noble and impressive.

This can be seen in my own company. I have set high expectations for my team's performance in achieving our mission, which is expressed as, "At TFS, we share and support our clients' passion for making a difference." My team owns this mission (which it also created) and sees tremendous value in it. It puts us on the same side of the field with our clients as we all try to accomplish the same goal, making a difference—they in the lives of their students or employees and we in our support function to attain their objective. It is that vision of the mission that drives higher expectations.

As a result, my team feels empowered and responsible for a shared TFS-client success, and they take ownership in the high-quality delivery of all our products and services. One of the ways I have had to adjust is allowing my team the freedom to work beyond the limits of a standard day. I have never required that they work outside the normal Monday through Friday workday hours, but my team works whenever is necessary to accomplish our shared mission. It is not uncommon to see numerous emails from my team at all hours of the evening, early morning, and throughout the weekend. I have a high percentage of Why Generation members on my team, and they don't simply accept, but embrace higher expectations for their performance and availability because of that shared mission and vision of what we are accomplishing in the world of education and workforce development.

Respect and How It Works Today

By far the biggest "aha" moment I have witnessed from audiences and clients alike in the past several years has been the realization that respect today works quite differently from how it did when I was young. When I was growing up, I respected my elders, teachers, and employers first and worked tirelessly to earn their respect.

Because society has changed so foundationally, Why Generation members aim it 180 degrees in the opposite direction: they require you respect them first, and then, and only then, will they mirror back that respect. Thankfully, the moment they feel that respect, they return it quickly.

Respect, defined by Merriam-Webster as "a feeling or under-standing that someone or something is important, serious, etc., and should be treated in an appropriate way," is shown in various ways depending on the relationship. For many, it boils down to listening seriously to the other person's perspective, avoiding high-handed treatment that underscores the recipient's subordinate or dependent position, making decisions based on consensus rather than arbitrary opinions, and believing that the other person has valuable contributions to make. If we show respect to young people, they will respond in kind. The key is to remember the order: respect that is first shown to Why Generation members will be reciprocated in their personal, educational, and professional interactions.

Older generations struggle with this realization and fight to demand respect as a given. That is simply a recipe for frustration and disappointment. Candidly, respect must be earned in both directions and can no longer be assumed.

Several years ago, I delivered a keynote address where I presented the facts about respect to a large audience. Eight months later I received a personal note from a teacher thanking me for the information on respect, saying it changed the way she interacted with her students and significantly improved student performance as a result. Ultimately, she didn't need to make sweeping reforms to reach her class; she simply needed to adjust the way she interacted and motivated her students while standing on common ground. She made students feel unique, special, and important—and that made all the difference. As their respect for her grew, so did their performance.

The Why Generation embodies the notion that "they do not care how much you know, until they know how much you care."

As I have said time and time again, experience is everything to this generation, and respect is a piece of that experience. Feeling respected and appreciated, combined with seeing the Light at the End of the Tunnel, fuels their imagination and desire for success.

Over the years, I have received many such notes from teachers, business and industry professionals, and organizations that have embraced the simple yet elusive concept that respect is the carrot that everyone wants. Regardless of age, it is that one thing we all desire and hunt for in one way, shape, or form.

Best Practices in Implementing the Career Tree

The Career Tree we introduced in chapter six is a powerful basis to start the ongoing career conversation with students and help them discover what they want to do in life—but it's just the foundation. The amazing teachers who utilize this strategy every day in their classrooms are creating the ongoing best practices and innovations that make working with the Tree a truly life-changing experience for their students. They do this by studying the unique needs of their students and program and then adapting the Tree to address these needs in fresh and dynamic ways. The Career Tree is truly a collaborative best practice that is continually growing more effective due to the grassroots vision and creativity of these educators and employers—particularly those striving to build a planning culture. As use of the Career Tree continues to expand throughout organizations internationally, these unique best practices will also continue to expand as these educators and employers share their successes. Here are some prime examples of how organizations are building a planning culture using the Career Tree.

CAREER TREE TUESDAYS

Every Tuesday, many of our partner schools make the Career Tree top of mind in all classrooms. Students use this time to go through the worksheets, give career presentations, talk through their branch choices, hear from industry experts, and participate in many more Career Tree activities. The Career Tree is used throughout the week, but this dedicated time block has been highly beneficial in keeping students (and staff) focused on the Light at the End of the Tunnel.

TREE WEEK

In addition to Career Tree Tuesdays, some of our clients also hold Tree Week in the fall and spring of each year. During Tree Week, the Career Tree is front and center in everything they do. Each program shares its most exciting pathways, student successes, projects, and career plans. There are Career Tree activities planned for each day as the whole organization focuses on growing students' opportunities and spreading awareness of the benefits of early career exploration.

CAREER PLAN OF THE WEEK AWARD

At many Career Tree organizations that have built a planning culture, students are encouraged to submit their career plan to win the Career Plan of the Week award. Each week's winning career plan is featured on the campus TV screens, social channels, and more. This sparks other students to think about their own career and life plans, helping them to set goals and begin achieving them.

PLAN A AND PLAN B

An instructor in Arizona has come up with a creative way to engage students in his program who may have career aspirations in a field different from his program. They put their Plan A career choice on the Tree, but also choose a Plan B career that is related to the program. For example, a student taking an automotive course may want to become a lawyer (Plan A) but also thinks automotive designer would be an interesting career (Plan B). Plan B motivates these students to do their best, making it worth their time and effort to perform well in the program. And they can then use Plan B to fund Plan A if they desire.

NETWORKING ROOTS

An Oklahoma teacher has created a networking activity as part of the Professional Skills and Experiences Roots of the Career Tree. Once a student has placed a Career Leaf on their desired branch, he or she must make contact with someone in that industry working that job. The student reaches out to this person to request a job shadowing opportunity to see what the experience is really like on an ordinary day. Students also invite their industry contact to the classroom to present to the class in a 30-minute talk (ideally 15 minutes for the presentation and 15 minutes for questions). This best practice not only teaches students how to function in professional interactions, but also sets them up for successful networking in the future.

YOUTUBE IT

An instructor at a Massachusetts school is using YouTube to help his students find their perfect branch. This best practice is simple: after he explains the Career Tree and sends students off to start their research on what might be their perfect branch, he instructs each student to email him a short two- to three-minute YouTube video that shows the chosen career branch. Not only does this deepen the student's career discovery process, it also gives this instructor a pool of short videos he can access at any time. These videos can be shown in class to highlight individual careers, shared with students who may be struggling to find their branch, and used with future classes as the pool of videos continues to grow. This simple best practice can be implemented at any point in the year, making it an easy way to maximize the Tree's impact for each student.

MARK IT UP, MAKE IT REAL

One instructor created a simple strategy to make the Tree's careers more real to students. On his interactive wall graphic, he adds a red mark next to the career branches that his program graduates have reached. With 36 careers listed, one program tree had 33 marks to show students where successful program completion could take them. This is also a powerful statement for program visitors, who can see not just the career aspirations of current students (represented by the leaves), but also the successful outcomes for program graduates. Showing a robust variety of careers on the Tree allows each teacher to tell the story that makes the benefits real to the audience.

SHINE THE LIGHT WITH PROGRAM GRADUATES

Keeping alumni engaged can pay dividends for current students, and a culinary program instructor understands the power of this tactic to engage and excite her students. This instructor once taught an ambitious young woman who graduated from the program and went on to get additional training. Eventually, this young woman won an Iron Chef competition to become one of the executive chefs at a prominent Las Vegas hotel. Over the years this young woman's instructor stayed in touch, and now this highly successful chef

Skypes in on the first day of school every year to talk to her former instructor's new class about what a culinary career is really like. She's shining the Light at the End of the Tunnel for these students, and they're always hooked. It sets the tone for the rest of the year, and it all began with that continuing alumnus-instructor relationship and connecting the dots for her new students.

CREATING CAREER CONVERSATIONS

Imagine an event where a school could host prospective students and their parents and talk about the truly amazing opportunities that are available to them—all with the help of the Career Tree to guide the process. It's quite a different picture from the traditional open house, isn't it? Similarly, what if you, as an employer, held an event where you could talk to prospective new employees about the kinds of careers available at your organization? Maybe not even the jobs you are hiring for now but rather the kinds that a new hire could aspire to given the right combination of skills, experience, and education. Even better, what if you found a way to have these kinds of conversations throughout the year instead of just once a year?

Traditional open houses or job fairs are usually passive (reactive): teachers or employers stand around waiting for people to walk up and ask what their program or organization is all about. This extremely broad question is tough to answer in 30 seconds. People may get distracted or bogged down in details—and walk away not sure about the value of enrolling in the program or working for the organization. Not to mention that a large turnout can actually cause more problems because visitors have to stand in line to talk to the instructor or company representative, who is now feeling the pressure of having to rush.

That's why creating more informal events to help stoke conversations about career opportunities takes a far more proactive approach to getting the right students or employees in the right programs or organizations for the right reasons. Career conversations are built around the experience of the program or pathway: demos, activities, testimonials from current students or employees, a structured path of stations and experiences, and of course, a clear picture of where the program or company can take them.

An effective career conversation answers every parent's burning question: "Why would my son or daughter do this?" I believe the best career conversations are those that help young people find their direction sooner so that they can invest in additional education wisely and purposefully. Far from limiting a young person's options, the goal of early career exploration actually expands opportunities for every post-graduation path: college, career, or advanced training. A great career conversation will highlight the competitive advantage that every young person brings, no matter what their education and career aspirations. Creating these conversations is also part of a larger planning culture that helps individuals thrive, both now and in their future. They help give students the critical foundation, relevance, and excitement to create effective goals and plans, share what they've established, collaborate with peers, and ultimately take action on their plan.

ACTIVATING ASPIRING ENTREPRENEURS

The Why Generation is shaping up to become one of the most entrepreneurial generational cohorts in our history. Many members of these generations have already made their mark through their "side hustles," small business gigs performed in the evenings or weekends alongside their regular jobs to bring in extra money and maybe pursue a passion that can't quite support full-time employment. With a Gallup poll indicating that nearly 80 percent want to be their own boss someday, we're going to see massive shifts in the workplace, the

training market, and the way young people approach their professional lives.[1]

There are many ways that we as educators and employers can
help these young entrepreneurs to achieve their aspirations. Programs and pathways that teach skills and allow career exploration
early on can:

- **Allow students to explore their interests and talents
  while in high school,** empowering them to discover
  what they love sooner so they can start preparing now.

- **Acquire the skills and industry knowledge that
  can make the difference for a young entrepreneur.**
  Internships, apprenticeships, maker spaces, and other
  hands-on opportunities are just a few of the ways
  young people can break into their field of interest.

- **Enable student-run enterprises that allow young
  people to actually work in and manage business
  environments** where they can pick up the knowledge
  that can only be received through experience.

- **Provide experiential learning that takes place both
  independently and in team contexts,** preparing students for entrepreneurial careers that involve lots of
  work by themselves as well as with others.

- **Acquire lifelong marketable skills that can help
  Why Generation members get on their feet
  financially and fund their independent business ventures.** Even if a program is not in the field
  they want to ultimately pursue, a lifelong marketable skill is a valuable asset in the uncertain realm of
  entrepreneurship.

With contextualized learning, hands-on experiences, high-demand focus areas, and opportunities for self-discovery and development, early exposure to skills training and career exploration is clearly poised to meet the pressing need of entrepreneur-minded students. Now is the moment to share a simple truth: exposing Why Generation members to these pathways gives them the tools to be their own boss. Let's get that message out there to inspire the next generation of movers and shakers.

The entrepreneurial bent of many Why Generation members also presents a great opportunity for companies to understand what makes them tick and how to capture their imagination as both consumers and contributors.

It's important to remember that it's not just about the money for these young people. Through their businesses and nonprofits, many entrepreneurial members of the Why Generation are seeking to solve social issues and needs. They want to use their professional lives to make the world a better place. That means it's more critical than ever for businesses to connect their offerings to a social vision of improving quality of life in some way for their communities, regions, and around the globe.

If your product or service is not directly marketable as a meaningful improvement for social conditions, there's a lot you can achieve through consistent community presence. Whether it's sponsoring community projects; participating in food, clothing, and blood drives; or any number of unique ways to make an impact, your company's involvement in the arena it serves is a powerful statement. It's all about giving back, and making this a core value will attract like-minded young people who admire that vision and want to take part in it.

For many, the attraction of running their own business is not necessarily in the business ownership itself, but in the flexibility and freedom they envision as part of that lifestyle. The rise of the work-life blend versus the work-life balance is a trend that companies will do well to embrace by giving their people as much autonomy as possible over work schedules and tasks. The light here for many younger workers is freedom from the traditional, rigid nine-to-five schedule and flexibility to perform their work at their pace and on their time. They'll get it done—because they believe in it.

But this is also why it's critical to think of members of the Why Generation as contributors rather than employees. The difference may be semantic (after all, if they work at your company they're technically your employees), but it also demonstrates your insight on how they view themselves on the job. They contribute their talents, ideas, abilities, and insights to your business in return for compensation, rather than merely performing assigned tasks as previous generations have done. Today, this perspective is foundational at companies that possess a strong recruitment and retention culture—where entrepreneurial-spirited young people experience the freedom to perform at their highest level.

CHAPTER NINE INSIGHTS

- Multiple strategies exist for parents, educators, and employers to rethink their approach to the young people of the Why Generation and activate their strengths. The strategies in this chapter are flexible enough to be adapted in a variety of settings such as the classroom, workplace, and home.

- Today's young people thrive when you can offer them a supportive work and learning environment while also presenting them with many challenges to rise to. The long-term, big-picture goal matters but must be broken down into smaller steps for maximum achievement.

- Instead of giving them rules, give Why Generation members tips for success as you position yourself as an ally in their experience. This is a key part of the supportive and structured learning and work environments they need to perform at their highest level.

- Give young people the chance to work in groups and to interact regularly with their peers. You can help enable this dynamic by embracing technology.

- Young people will rise to the level of expectations you place on them. Too often, they don't expect enough of themselves. Help unlock their potential by giving them lofty goals they can embrace.

- The respect relationship works differently today. Why Generation members must feel respected before they will reciprocate that respect.

- Strategies like Career Tree Tuesdays, Tree Week, the Career Plan of the Week Award, and others are part of an overarching planning culture where goal-setting and planning are the norm for students to succeed.

- The Why Generation might be the most entrepreneurial group of people on the planet. Embrace that by giving young people the chance to learn the skills early on that will make them successful in their pursuits.

The Wade Factor

One day several years ago, I met a remarkable man who taught me more than anyone else ever has about what it really means to implement all the knowledge we have. His name was Wade and he was driving a rental car bus from the Baltimore Airport to the off-site rental car center located about 10 minutes away. As part of my plan that day, I was traveling to Washington, DC, for a 3:00 p.m. meeting and had decided to fly into Baltimore in the early morning, rent a car, and drive to Annapolis for a brief stop before continuing on to my DC meeting. Best-laid plans.

It was snowing with occasional near white-out conditions in Cleveland that Friday morning, hampering flight and ground operations at Cleveland Hopkins Airport. The weather caused an extended delay in our departure for Baltimore, and we arrived at the Baltimore Airport over four hours late. Anxious to start the drive to DC to make the meeting on time, or at least only minutes behind schedule, I was stressed and challenged and was not in the most cheerful of moods. Enter Wade. Without even knowing it, he was going to be remarkably calming and inspiring to me that day. Wade was warm, charming, funny, and passionate about life. He exuded confidence and truly cared about the people he was transporting—I could feel it from the moment I met him. I don't know if he was trained on how to connect with people effectively in his work context or if his skills were instinctual, but however he attained that knowledge, he put it to work in every interaction. To this day Wade is one of the most remarkable people I have ever met.

As I was standing on the curb outside the airport with my business colleague that day, the rental car bus rolled to a stop and Wade jumped off the bus. Now when I say he jumped off the bus, I mean he had a real passion in his step. He looked us both square in the eye and said, "Glad you both made it here safely! Let me grab your bags while you both get comfortable inside the bus." As a true road warrior, I was taken by surprise. I am rarely met with such warmth and enthusiasm for one's job. It was refreshing, and I recall liking Wade immediately.

We stepped inside the bus, which was long, crowded, uncomfortable, and in a U-shaped configuration where you could sit on either side of the bus or in the very back, but regardless all the passengers had to face each other. You have likely sat on this kind of bus at some point in your life, so you can appreciate the typical demeanor of the travelers inside. The goal of the trip is to not have personal interaction with anyone. Each person either looks down at the floor or out the window with a glassy stare or reads the propaganda on the signs—but making eye contact is unthinkable. It's what I lovingly refer to as "the voyage of the damned."

Wade was roughly 28–30 years old and had a clear, deep voice that commanded attention when he spoke. As he pulled away from the curb, he got on the microphone to say, "Good afternoon, my name is Wade, and I will be driving you out to the rental car facility today. Thank you for making Baltimore your final stop today, and I want you to know that whatever stresses and challenges have brought you to this moment, I want you to take a deep breath and I want you to relax—because I've got you and I want to ensure I give you enough information to help expedite your trip through the rental car facility."

He paused . . . and you could literally see people take a deep breath and exhale. He then went on to tell two of the funniest jokes I have ever heard. They were short and sweet and everyone burst out laughing in a full-belly-laugh kind of reaction. He was funny! I wish I could remember the jokes; I would include them right here. He then gave us a few quick and helpful tips for when we arrived at the facility and stopped talking.

Now, in the back of the bus, it's like Mardi Gras. When you have laughed with people, the veil of secrecy is gone. We all had common ground—we had all laughed at the same jokes and had a shared sense of what was funny. Suddenly our newfound friends were sharing jokes that were similar, so the laughter roared on. Everyone was involved and engaged in the ride to the facility. Several more jokes and more laughter ensued. It was fun, enjoyable, and stress relieving. As the laughter started to die down, the conversations started. We now became friends. We became genuinely interested in the other people that only moments earlier we had wanted nothing to do with. Where eye contact had been unthinkable, it now became preferred.

Where are you headed? How long will you be in town? Where are you from? How delayed was your flight? These are just a few of the questions that flew back and forth among people who now enjoyed each other's company and interaction. This was a remarkable transformation in a 10-minute journey with complete strangers, and Wade was the catalyst for all of it. His positive attitude, engaging demeanor, and genuine warmth made this possible.

About a minute before we arrived at the facility, Wade got back on the microphone to say, "Thank you again for making Baltimore your final stop today, and I want to encourage those of you that did not bring family with you on this trip, please visit again soon—we have such a family-friendly city with the Inner Harbor, Aquarium . . ." and a few other attractions I do not recall.

He went on, "I am about to come to a stop in front of the rental car facility, so any of you that wish to grab your bags and go, please feel like you can do that. But for anyone needing assistance, I am here to help get you safely on your way." He then closed with one more brief and funny witticism, and everyone burst out laughing as we jumped to our feet and began exiting the bus while saying our goodbyes and offering best wishes. It was extraordinary and in some ways magical.

Have you ever met someone who put a bounce in your step, made you feel better, or seemed to remove the chip from your shoulder? That was Wade. Despite all that had occurred to bring me to Wade's bus—the travel delays, meeting time pressure, and stress of making the day work—it all seemed to melt away after that 10-minute ride. Wade unlocked in each of us that guarded enthusiasm, fun personality, and deep-seated desire to connect with others that we all had been hiding from view. Wade made us feel better about ourselves and our circumstances, and ultimately made a tremendous difference for those around him.

In the process, he was a remarkable ambassador for the city of Baltimore. He radiated pride for his city, his job, and himself. I've been back to Baltimore many times since that trip and I have never seen another bus driver do this nor have I seen Wade again. In fact, the bus microphone has been replaced with automated messages throughout the journey. Wade's interaction that day was pure quintessential Wade; he did the things he did not because he had to, but because he wanted to make a difference in your journey. He put his skills into action.

As my colleague and I departed that bus, we felt great about our shared experience and sported huge smiles which lasted a full 60 seconds until we walked up to the Avis counter, where we met the person I affectionately refer to as the anti-Wade. Boom! Back to reality. Her name was April, and maybe because it was January it was just not April's month. To her credit she got us in and out of the rental transaction in three short minutes. Have you ever seen someone whirl so fast on a keyboard that you wonder whether in fact they are actually typing? I will never forget her long nails clicking on the keys like she was sending Morse code to a Russian trawler off the coast of Baltimore.

During our brief three-minute interaction, she was cold, standoffish, and even flat-out rude. She never looked up at me from her computer or acknowledged me in any way except to rap out, "Name?!" She was technically proficient, but when it came to making a connection with people—not so much. I walked away from that fleeting unpleasant exchange in awe that within 60 seconds I could meet two people so diametrically opposed. To walk from Wade to April and see both ends of the spectrum in such juxtaposition was astounding. April clearly missed the fact that Avis spends millions of dollars to bring me to the point of renting their car. And where the rubber literally meets the road—she gets handed the ball, and she doesn't just drop it. She destroys it.

The point of this story is for us to ask ourselves whether we are more like Wade or more like April. Are our families, friends, organizations, and communities mostly made up of Wades or Aprils? Are we making creative use of all the knowledge and strategies we have learned over the course of our careers and life experiences, or have we set them aside in favor of just getting through the task at hand? Wade didn't do that; he was fully present, engaged, and using his people skills to the fullest degree even in a context so seemingly trivial as a 10-minute bus ride from the airport. Are we giving the "trivial" interactions and situations in our lives the same level of engagement? Wade knew how to connect and create common ground with those around him. He put us at ease because he made it clear he knew where we were going and was prepared to share insights on what to do when we got there—which is the foundation for Light at the End of the Tunnel.

We all lean toward one end of the Wade-April spectrum or the other. I can guarantee that the messages you are sending, personally and professionally, are being received whether you realize it or not. As an illustration of that point, I was once doing a two-hour presentation at the Chicago Public Schools. I always end my keynote presentations with the Wade Factor story, as I find it a compelling call to action for individuals and organizations to truly make a bigger difference in their relationships, interactions, and day-to-day travels. We have it within ourselves to be more like Wade and touch people in a positive, warm, and genuine way that makes lives better—it simply takes the desire to impact people in that way and use the information we already have to do it.

At the Chicago Public Schools I was presenting in a large room with about 275 administrators from roughly 76 metro high schools—a great group. At the end, I took 30 minutes of questions and answers, and the last question blew me away. The question was this: "Does Wade know that you talk about him in your speeches?" The answer is no, Wade has no idea. Think about this . . . Wade has no clue that on a routine day, during a trip to a rental car center that he had made hundreds if not thousands of times, he so deeply influenced one traveler, me, that I have published an article about him in a national magazine, have shared his story at the end of every keynote address for many years, and have now included his story in this book. Hundreds of thousands of people have already heard about Wade—and he has no idea it is happening. (So, too, April has no idea that her name has become a five-letter expletive for poor customer service.)

Imagine the sheer magnitude of one 10-minute encounter positively affecting an awe-inspiring number of people nationwide—simply through one man's optimistic outlook and genuine nature. Imagine how your life can impact those around you and the vast ripple effects that can flow far beyond your direct interactions or those of your children, students, employees, and community. I am keenly aware that every time I speak at educational conferences, the audience is made up of administrators, teachers, and critical support staff members who have the ability to alter the way they influence students' lives. For every educator I can influence, they can influence countless students, who go on to influence all the people in their lives. The ripple effect can turn us all from a single drip to a powerful wave. So as a nation, is our goal to inspire more Wades—and Aprils—by helping them to find the path that gets them to their Light at the End of the Tunnel? How can we, as educators and employers, help make the connection for young people so they can make the most of their unique interests, talents, and abilities?

It's so simple but so profound: Wade actually *used* the knowledge he had to connect with everyone who crossed his path, creating common ground with them. He valued people and he gave his best effort on that routine bus ride, on a normal day, with a group of people who needed his help. And that's what I want to challenge you to do.

In this book I have shared tons of information and insights about the Why Generation. But none of it will make a difference if we don't implement it. It's not enough to read this book and give a nod of agreement; we must be committed to using its insights in our daily interactions if they are to have any effect.

If we can implement this knowledge, the opportunity is enormous. I'm talking about our opportunity right here and now to help our students become truly career ready, equipped, and eager to compete in a new global economy. This is more than just education policy rhetoric; our expanding national skills gap makes it a burning necessity.

I've devoted my career to helping young people perform at their highest potential, and I know that the young people that make up the Why Generation have it within themselves to be the next greatest generation. They're tenacious and talented, but they need to be motivated to reach their peak performance. They can do it—but we have to help.

We have to get beyond how we have stigmatized non-college career paths, as if those individuals who choose them are pursuing lesser dreams than their college-bound counterparts. With the best of intentions, we as a nation are doing our young people—and our economy—a grave disservice.

I urge you to take the time to discover the many diverse pathways to successful careers that are open to the Why Generation in our changing world. We must promote awareness of these pathways and careers that go beyond the traditional college route. Together, we can advocate for meaningful, structured career exploration in our middle and high schools so that our young people can graduate with a plan and the perseverance to see it through. We can help them unleash their innate passion, purpose, and performance—and this is our moment to make a difference, both for the Why Generation today and for the generations to follow. Let's take it!

The call to action for all of us is clear. We must tirelessly communicate to students, parents, and communities about the many worthwhile pathways young people can take after high school graduation. We must show them these choices in many different ways, demonstrating the successful journeys of our program alumni, integrating powerful career exploration and plans of study into our curriculum, and extolling the value of all postsecondary pathways.

I know, maybe it sounds like a daunting challenge. The branch is creaking big time. But you know what the good news is? We can do something about it as a nation because, as you might remember, we have dealt with branch creaks before.

So What Can You Do?

As I sit and contemplate how I want to end this book, I keep coming back to a simple question: do you hear the branch creaking like I do when it comes to the Why Generation? If you do, will you focus, plan, and take action? Or will you just cling to the branch and hope it doesn't give way beneath us all?

If you're stuck somewhere in between, let me share one last story that I hope might inspire you.

One of my favorite movies of all time is *Apollo 13*. I loved seeing it on the big screen. The launch sequence still gives me chills, as it is the perfect cinematic crossroad of realism, live action, computer graphics, sound effects, and a musical score that clutches your heart and takes you for a ride inside the capsule of the *Apollo 13* ship. Exhilarating!

I have always been captivated and astonished by our discovery of space and the courageous men and women who have explored the new frontier, both those inside the capsule and those supporting the mission from the ground. This was a true triumph of teamwork, collaboration, and innovation that made the July 20, 1969, moon landing of *Apollo 11* and subsequent first walk on the moon a source of great national attention and pride. The nation was mesmerized by the coverage, watching breathlessly as Neil Armstrong and Buzz Aldrin made those first historic steps on the surface of the moon. The real-life *Apollo 13* was to be the third landing on the moon in April 1970 following the successful *Apollo 12* moon landing just five months earlier.

The movie *Apollo 13* was everything I hoped it would be . . . thrilling, realistic, and accurate in its portrayal of three brave men hearing a tremendous branch creak of life-threatening proportions on that fateful day when part of their spacecraft's Service Module (SM) oxygen tank no. 2 exploded, crippling their spacecraft. "Houston, we have a problem . . . ," as mission Commander Jim Lovell, played by actor Tom Hanks, put it. To watch the ensuing chain of events that transpired during the following 15 minutes to keep the crew alive is extraordinary. The three astronauts and all of Mission Control worked at a furious pace to focus, plan, and take immediate action.

It was swiftly determined they would need to utilize their Lunar Excursion Module (or LEM) as a lifeboat to circle the moon and return safely to Earth. In a matter of minutes they needed to power up the LEM and power down the Command Module (CM) as they were transferring critical computer guidance information from the CM to the LEM. Energy was running critically low, they were bleeding oxygen, and they were running out of precious time—time they could not afford to lose. The entire mission was fraught with challenges that needed to be solved, and on April 17, 1970, after a harrowing five days and just under 23 hours in space, the spacecraft returned safely to the warm waters of the South Pacific.

As a result of seeing this movie, I have always placed dinner with its director Ron Howard on the top of my bucket list, as I value his unique ability to tell an important story and involve the audience in the events on screen. This movie came at a time when I needed inspiration, and I found it that day in the theater in the form of my favorite movie line of all time. In fact, after hearing the line, I left the theater and emblazoned it above my desk. It has driven me almost every day since 1995. It's not the one people would normally guess, which would be the famous line of Gene Krantz, as played by actor Ed Harris: "We've never lost an American in space; we're sure as hell not gonna lose one on my watch! Failure is not an option."

No, my favorite line comes at the beginning of the movie. It's July

20, 1969, and Neil Armstrong and Buzz Aldrin are getting ready to walk on the surface of the moon for the first time. Jim Lovell and his wife are throwing a party at their home in Houston to watch the historic event. They have lots of guests and the champagne is on ice. The line that has had such an impact on me is spoken at the end of the evening when the guests have departed and the Lovells are sitting outside in lounge chairs, beer cans strewn on the ground, looking up at the moon. Tom Hanks playing Jim Lovell says this: "From now on we live in a world where man has walked on the moon. It wasn't a miracle; we just decided to go."

"It wasn't a miracle; we just decided to go." I find that sentence to be the most promising words I have ever heard. To understand their significance we have to back up to May 25, 1961, when John F. Kennedy stood before a joint session of Congress and committed the nation, by the end of the decade, to landing a man on the moon and returning him safely to Earth. Just over eight years later, on July 20, 1969, we realized that goal. "It wasn't a miracle; we just decided to go." To accomplish that feat, hundreds of thousands of Americans worked tirelessly to create things that had never been built before. They needed to invent, design, build, and test everything—each system, instrument, and component right down to each screw.

At the time Kennedy made that speech we didn't know how to get there. We had not settled on Earth Orbit Rendezvous, Lunar Orbit Rendezvous, one spacecraft or multiple, or how we would solve the challenge of the Space Race. The clock was ticking and the nation was engaged. "It wasn't a miracle; we just decided to go."

We have accomplished so much as a nation, a people, and as individuals. It became a source of great inspiration to understand that we can accomplish anything—especially when we work together. We simply need to make the decision to go.

Whether you're an educator working with the Why Generation every day, a parent struggling with the demands of rearing a Why

Generation member, an employer building an engaged and empowered workforce that takes ownership for a job well done, or a person in a leadership role on a local, state, or national level—I encourage you to consider the strategies conveyed within these pages. We all want the same thing: a way to unleash the young people of the Why Generation so they can perform exceptionally. I know these strategies work because I've seen the transformation through the stories of countless parents, students, teachers, employees, and employers I have listened to throughout my travels. We can all be more like Wade and choose to daily implement the knowledge we have gained.

When the branch creaks, we can make a tremendous difference if we choose to. And it doesn't require a miracle. We just have to make the decision to go.

Maximize your experience of *Answering Why* with the complimentary discussion guide at MarkCPerna.com

Deepen your understanding of *Answering Why*'s message and strategies with this useful resource for both individuals and groups. Through in-depth questions for each chapter, this discussion guide empowers you to explore the book's concepts and apply its principles.

Visit MarkCPerna.com to download your *Answering Why* discussion guide and take your knowledge to the next level!

Acknowledgments

This book has benefited from the perspectives and wisdom of so many generous individuals. I can't possibly thank them all here, but my gratitude is no less for the inspiration they have shared with me.

To my remarkable team at TFS—Kristy Warrell, Greg Scheetz, Tom Schultz, Christine Feigl, Matthew Perna, and Amy Timco—thank you for your unconditional support and creativity. I'm incredibly proud of the work we do together. Also, special thanks to Amy for always being there with the right word, phrase, and perspective when I need one.

To my visionary clients, thank you for being the "proving ground" where my strategies and tools were first unveiled. I'm privileged to work with you to make a bigger difference for young people today.

My amazing family and friends have supported me throughout this project with constructive feedback, helpful suggestions, and untiring interest. You encouraged and challenged me at every step, and this book is better for it. Please know how deeply grateful I am for all the ways you enrich my life.

I'm thankful to my team at Greenleaf for believing in me and the vision of this book's narrative. I especially appreciate my editorial team, led by AprilJo Murphy, for their input and buzz-killing reality when I needed to change direction in an earlier version of the manuscript. My thanks also to Darren Dahl for his support in organizing the material and helping me create additional connections between the different sections of the book.

Thank you to my PR and social media team for getting the word out about my work and vision to a larger audience.

And finally, thank you to my sons, Matthew and Nicholas, for providing me with an unmatched opportunity to truly understand the Why Generation—at home, at school, and at work. I couldn't have written this book without the lessons you taught me.

Endnotes

Introduction

1. Personal communication with the author.

2. Niraj Chokshi, "How badly companies misunderstand millennials," *The Washington Post* (May 11, 2016), https://www.washingtonpost.com/news/wonk/wp/2016/05/11/how-badly-companies-misunderstand-millennials/.

3. Deloitte, "The 2017 Deloitte Millennial Survey," *Deloitte* (2017), http://www2.deloitte.com/global/en/pages/about-deloitte/articles/millennialsurvey.html.

4. Kim Clark, "A Record Number of People Aren't Paying Back Their Student Loans," *Money* (March 14, 2017), http://time.com/money/4701506/student-loan-defaults-record-2016/.

Chapter One

1. EdSurge, "NMC Report Addresses Barriers to Graduation," *EdSurge* (October 28, 2016), https://www.edsurge.com/news/2016-10-28-nmc-report-addresses-barriers-to-graduation.

2. Kevin Fleming, "Success in the New Economy," YouTube video, 9:35, posted by Substance Media Inc (January 28, 2015), https://www.youtube.com/watch?v=zs6nQpVI164.

3. Eric Risberg, "Half of new graduates are jobless or underemployed," *USA Today* (April 23, 2012), http://usatoday30.usatoday.com/news/nation/story/2012-04-22/college-grads-jobless/54473426/1.

4. Greg St. Martin, "Generation Z and The Future of Higher Education," *Northeastern* (November 19, 2014), http://news. northeastern.edu/2014/11/generation-z-and-the-future-of-higher -education/.

5. Sparks & Honey, "Meet Generation Z: Forget Everything You Learned About Millennials," *SlideShare* (June 17, 2014), https:// www.slideshare.net/sparksandhoney/generation-z-final-june-17/28 -They_multitask_across_5_screens.

6. Elizabeth Chuck, "Just Over Half of All College Students Actually Graduate, Reports Find," *NBC News* (November 18, 2015), http:// www.nbcnews.com/feature/freshman-year/just-over-half-all-college -students-actually-graduate-report-finds-n465606.

7. Phone interview.

8. Phone interview.

9. Phone interview.

10. Kaitlin Mulhere, "One Quarter of College Grads are Overqualified for Their Jobs," *Money* (February 2, 2017), http://time.com/ money/4658059/college-grads-workers-overqualified-jobs/.

11. Personal communication with the author.

12. Attn:, "In Germany, learning a trade is just as valuable as a college education. –Mike Rowe," Facebook video, 1:30, posted by Attn: (August 24, 2017) https://www.facebook.com/attn/ videos/1481545225214265/.

13. Association for Career & Technical Education (ACTE), "About CTE," *ACTE*, https://www.acteonline.org/aboutcte/#. WdVHzVtSzDd.

Chapter Two

1. Stephen R. Covey, *The 7 Habits of Highly Effective People: Restoring the Character Ethic*, New York: Free Press (2004).

2. Brigid Schulte, "Millennials are actually more generous than anybody realizes," *Washington Post* (June 24, 2015), https://www. washingtonpost.com/news/wonk/wp/2015/06/24/millennials-are -actually-more-generous-than-anybody-realizes/.

Chapter Three

1. Lauren Martin, "50 Things About Millennials That Make Corporate America Sh*t Its Pants," *Elite Daily* (Sept. 16, 2014), http://elitedaily.com/life/50-things-millennials-make-corporate-america-uncomfortable/758330/.

2. Sparks & Honey, "Meet Generation Z: Forget Everything You Learned About Millennials," *SlideShare* (June 17, 2014), http://www.slideshare.net/sparksandhoney/generation-z-final-june-17/36-36They_love_the_ephemeral_and.

3. Ron Alsop, "The 'Trophy' Kids Go to Work," *The Wall Street Journal* (Oct. 21 2008), https://www.wsj.com/articles/SB122455219391652725.

4. Personal conversation through an interview.

5. Lauren Martin, "50 Things About Millennials That Make Corporate America Sh*t Its Pants," *Elite Daily* (Sept. 16 2014), http://elitedaily.com/life/50-things-millennials-make-corporate-america-uncomfortable/758330/.

6. Nadira A. Hira, "The Making of a UPS Driver," *Fortune* (November 7, 2007).

7. Niraj Chokshi, "How badly companies misunderstand millennials," *The Washington Post* (May 11, 2016), https://www.washingtonpost.com/news/wonk/wp/2016/05/11/how-badly-companies-misunderstand-millennials/.

8. Sue Dodsworth, "Creating a Millennial-Friendly Workplace: Tips from Kimberly-Clark," *Industry Week* (May 16, 2017), http://www.industryweek.com/recruiting-retention/creating-millennial-friendly-workplace-tips-kimberly-clark.

9. Ibid.

Chapter Four

1. Personal communication with the author.

2. Claudia Wallis, "To err is human – and a powerful prelude to learning," *The Hechinger Report* (July 26, 2017), http://hechingerreport.org/getting-errors-all-wrong/.

3. Personal communication with the author.

4. Personal communication with the author.

Chapter Five

1. Personal communication with the author.

Chapter Six

1. Personal communication with the author.

2. Personal communication with the author.

Chapter Eight

1. Purdue, "Contextual Teaching and Learning: What Is It?" *Purdue,* https://www.ydae.purdue.edu/lct/HBCU/documents/ ContextualTeachingandLearning.pdf.

2. Edgar Dale, "Cone of Learning," revised by Bruce Hyland, *Triton* (1969), https://www.triton.edu/uploadedFiles/Content/Academics/ Continuing_Education/Cone_of_Learning.pdf.

3. Natalie Saaris, "The Benefits of Deeper Learning: Retention, Transfer and Motivation," *Actively Learn* (June 30, 2017), https:// www.activelylearn.com/post/the-benefits-of-deeper-learning -retention-transfer-and-motivation.

4. Personal communication with the author.

5. Ashlee Kieler, "Two-Thirds of College Students Who Take Out Loans Have No Idea What They're In For," *Consumerist* (September 29, 2016), https://consumerist.com/2016/06/28/two -thirds-of-college-students-who-take-out-loans-have-no-idea-what -theyre-in-for/.

6. Julia Glum, "Student Debt Crisis 2016: New Graduates Owe a Record-Breaking Average $37,00 In Loans," *International Business Times* (May 6, 2016), http://www.ibtimes.com/student-debt -crisis-2016-new-graduates-owe-record-breaking-average-37000 -loans-2365195.

7. Terri Williams, "Only 1 in 5 Students Feel Prepared for Today's Job Market," *GoodCall* (June 9, 2015), https://www.goodcall.com/news/only-1-in-5-students-feel-prepared-for-todays-job-market-according-to-recent-study-01077.

8. U.S. Chamber of Commerce Foundation, "Changing the Debate on Quality Assurance in Higher Education," *U.S. Chamber of Commerce Foundation* (Accessed 7/26/2016), https://www.uschamberfoundation.org/sites/default/files/media-uploads/Changing%20the%20Debate%20draft.pdf.

9. Personal communication with the author.

Chapter Nine

1. Valerie J. Calderon, "U.S Students' Entrepreneurial Energy Waiting to Be Tapped," *Gallup* (October 13, 2011), http://www.gallup.com/poll/150077/students-entrepreneurial-energy-waiting-tapped.aspx.

Index

A

ABC (Associated Builders and Contractors), 80–81
action stage (creaking-branch metaphor), 163–65. *See also* Career Tree; Education with Purpose
  defined, 2
  overview, 12
ADD (attention deficit disorder), 95–96
Aldrin, Buzz, 207
alumni, keeping engaged, 191–92
Apollo 11, 207
Apollo 13 (film), 207–9
Armstrong, Neil, 207
Art and Performing Arts Career Tree, 121–22
  Entry-Level Careers, 121
  Professional Careers, 122
  Technical Careers, 122
Associated Builders and Contractors (ABC), 80–81
attention deficit disorder (ADD), 95–96

"authentic tasks", 165
Automotive Career Tree, 118–21, 148–50
  Entry-Level Careers, 119
  Professional Careers, 120–21
  Technical Careers, 120
Awareness Gap. *See also* Career Tree
  bridging, 107–11
  career exploration and, 140, 160
  choosing level of education needed for career goals, 18–22
  expectations, 185–86
  overview, 3–4
  of parents, 80–81
  role of parents in bridging, 79, 83

B

Baby Boom Generation
  Generational Rifts, 36, 37–38
  workplace expectations, 53
best practices (Career Tree), 188–96
  activating entrepreneurs, 193–96
  career conversations, 192–93

Career Plan of the Week award,
     189
Career Tree Tuesdays, 189
     interactive wall graphic, 191
     keeping alumni engaged, 191–92
     networking roots, 190
     overview, 188
     Plan A career, 189–90
     Plan B career, 190
     Tree Week, 189
     YouTube It, 190–91
Brokaw, Tom, 9, 37

C

career and technical education (CTE)
     programs, 27–29, 79
career exploration. *See also* Education
     with Purpose
     career conversations, 192–93
     career counseling, 166
     CTE programs, 27–29, 79
Career Plan of the Week award, 189
Career Tree
     adult learners use of, 131
     art and performing arts, 121–22
     automotive, 118–21
     best practices, 188–96
         activating entrepreneurs,
             193–96
         career conversations, 192–93
         Career Plan of the Week
             award, 189
         Career Tree Tuesdays, 189
         interactive wall graphic, 191
         keeping alumni engaged,
             191–92
         networking roots, 190
         overview, 188

Plan A career, 189–90
Plan B career, 190
Tree Week, 189
YouTube It, 190–91
county government and law,
     123–24
education, 122–23
Education with Purpose and,
     174–76
Entry-Level Careers, 114–15, 117
filmmaking and video production,
     125–26
health science, 124–25
Light at the End of the Tun-
     nel motivational strategy and,
     132–35
Manufacturing, 152–53
math, 126–27
overview, 111–14, 136–37
power of, 130–31
Professional Careers, 116, 117
Root System, 142–47
sports medicine and personal
     training, 127–28
teacher/student relationship and,
     151
Technical Careers, 115, 117
welding, 128–29
Career Tree Tuesdays, 189
challenges, as motivational tool, 180
Chokshi, Niraj, 58
college. *See also* Education with
     Purpose
     bridging the Awareness Gap,
         79–80, 109–10
     as career exploration, 20
     career-minded education before,
         140–41

college and career ready concept, 19

college-only mindset, 21–22

expectation and educational paradigm, 7–8, 18–19

Nick's story, 95–101

student loan debt, 18, 169–70

competitive advantage, building

growing opportunities, 147–52

manufacturing industry, 152–53

overview, 139–42

planning process, 154–59

Root System, 142–47

"Cone of Learning" (Dale), 164

contextual learning, 163–65, 177, 195

Cortés, Hernán, 91

County Government and Law Career Tree, 123–24

Entry-Level Careers, 123–24

Professional Careers, 124

Technical Careers, 124

Covey, Stephen R., 39

creaking-branch metaphor

action stage, 2, 12

Awareness Gap, 3–4

danger of safety nets, 67–71

educational funding and, 7

focus stage, 1, 11

Generational Rifts, 7

national branch creaks, 8–11

overview, 1–2

parenting and, 71–75

helicopter parents, 72–73

neglect, 74–75

overview, 71–72

power of failure, 76–81

strategic planning stage, 1–2, 11–12

TFS company perspective, 5–7

Why Generation, 4–5

CTE (career and technical education) programs, 27–29, 79

Cuyahoga Valley Career Center (CVCC), 97–98

D

Dale, Edgar, 164

dating environment, 49–50

Dirty Jobs (TV show), 26

dreams, building, 102–4, 105

drug use, 26–27, 74

Drury, Mark, 3

E

education. *See also* college; Education with Purpose

choosing level of education needed for career goals, 18–22

college and career ready concept, 19

expectation and educational paradigm, 18–19

student loan debt, 18, 169–70

supportive education and work environment, 180–81

Education Career Tree, 122–23

Entry-Level Careers, 122

Professional Careers, 123

Technical Careers, 123

Education with Purpose, 163–77

career ready concept, 169–71

Career Tree strategy, 174–76

contextual learning, 163–65, 177

defined, 177

Employment with Passion, 168–69, 177

focus stage, 170–71

Light at the End of the Tunnel
motivational strategy, 171–74,
178

overview, 165–68

planning culture philosophy, 168,
172, 177

employers
butt-kissing approach of, 57–60
changes in loyalty of, 60–61
partnering with Why Generation,
53–54
use of Internet in hiring decisions,
46–47

Employment with Passion, 168–69,
177

entitled mindset
development of, 69
Why Generation, 51–57, 63

entrepreneurial spirit
activating entrepreneurs, 193–96
Why Generation, 61

Entry-Level Careers
Art and Performing Arts Career
Tree, 121
Automotive Career Tree, 119
County Government and Law
Career Tree, 123–24
Education Career Tree, 122
Filmmaking and Video Produc-
tion Career Tree, 125–26
Health Science Career Tree,
124–25
Manufacturing Career Tree, 152
Math Career Tree, 126–27
overview, 114–15, 117
Sports Medicine and Personal
Training Career Tree, 127–28
Welding Career Tree, 128–29

expectations
expectation and educational paradigm, 7–8, 18–19
Generational Rifts, 38–39, 44
as motivational tool, 185–86
workplace, 51–57

experience-is-everything concept,
45–47, 63

experiential learning, 194

F

Facebook, 46

failure, power of, 76–81, 82

Filmmaking and Video Production
Career Tree, 125–26
Entry-Level Careers, 125–26
Professional Careers, 126
Technical Careers, 126

Fleming, Kevin, 16–17, 166

focus stage (creaking-branch
metaphor)
defined, 1
Education with Purpose and,
170–71
overview, 11
Why Generation, 51

Fortune 100 Executives, insights from,
22–29

Franklin, Benjamin, 164

friends, importance of to Why Generation, 46

G

Galbenski, Paul, 20, 21, 130–31, 171,
174

generational disconnect, 40–43

generational profiles, 37–40

Generational Rifts, 33–44. *See also*
Why Generation

Baby Boom Generation, 36, 37–38
defined, 7, 44
expectations, 38–39, 44
generational disconnect, 40–43
generational profiles, 37–40
Generation X, 36
Greatest Generation, 36, 37
Light at the End of the Tunnel motivational strategy, 39, 40
"live to work" creed, 40–42
Lost Generation, 36
overview, 33–34
Silent Generation, 36
stereotypes, 38
Why Generation, 34–36, 38, 40, 44
work-life blend, 41–43
"work to live" creed, 40–42
Generation X, 19, 36
Generation Y, 4. *See also* Why Generation
Generation Z, 4, 34. *See also* Why Generation
goal-setting, 85. *See also* Light at the End of the Tunnel motivational strategy
Greatest Generation, 36, 37
The Greatest Generation (Brokaw), 37
Great Recession, 80
Greene, Jimmy, 21–22, 26, 28
group dynamic (Why Generation), 49–50

H

Hanks, Tom, 208, 209
hard skills, 16
Harris, Ed, 208

Health Science Career Tree, 124–25
Entry-Level Careers, 124–25
Professional Careers, 125
Technical Careers, 125
helicopter parenting, 72–73, 82
Hickam, Homer, 9–10
Howard, Ron, 208
Hulu, 51

I

individuality, sense of, 48–49
Instagram, 46
interactive relationships, as motivational tool, 181–84

J

job fairs, 192
job-hopping, 5
Jumpstart Training Program, 80

K

Kennedy, John F., 209
Kimberly-Clark company, 58, 63–64
Krantz, Gene, 208

L

Light at the End of the Tunnel motivational strategy, 39, 40, 58, 75, 85–105
building dreams, 105
Career Tree and, 132–35, 137
defined, 105
Education with Purpose and, 171–74, 178
lessons learned as single parent, 86–94
"Living the Dream" speech, 102–4

overview, 85–86

"want-to," "how-to" concept,
    94–101
    defined, 105
    Nick's story, 95–101
    overview, 94–95
"live to work" creed, 40–42
"Living the Dream" speech, 102–4
Lost Generation, 36
Lovell, Jim, 208, 209
loyalty in workplace, 60–61, 64

M

Manufacturing Career Tree
    Entry-Level Careers, 152
    Professional Careers, 153
    Technical Careers, 153
manufacturing industry
    changes in, 23–24
    Manufacturing Career Tree,
        152–53
    perception of careers in, 25–26
marijuana use, 26
marine electrician, 156–57
Martinez, Michelle, 19–20, 167–68
Math Career Tree, 126–27
    Entry-Level Careers, 126–27
    Professional Careers, 127
    Technical Careers, 127
millennials, 34
'the mom factor', overcoming, 79
motivation. *See also* Light at the End
    of the Tunnel motivational strategy
multitasking, 51

N

national branch creaks, 8–11
neglect, effect on development, 74–75

Netflix, 51
Networking Roots, 190
non-college career paths, stigmatization
    of, 206

O

Oakland County Public Schools, 171
October Sky (film), 10
1:2:7 ratio, 17, 30
online presence, of Why Generation,
    46–47
"open book" philosophy, 46
open houses, 192
Orth, Jim, 133

P

"pack dating", 49–50
parenting, 71–75
    helicopter parents, 72–73, 82
    neglect, 74–75
    overview, 71–72
Perna, Matt, 86–93
Perna, Nick, 86–93, 95–101, 141–42
Pinterest, 46
Plan A career, 189–90
Plan B career, 190
planning culture philosophy, 133–35,
    137. *See also* Education with
    Purpose
priorities of Why Generation, 42–43,
    45, 48–49
privacy, differing views of, 46, 48
Professional Careers
    Art and Performing Arts Career
        Tree, 122
    Automotive Career Tree, 120–21
    County Government and Law
        Career Tree, 124

Education Career Tree, 123

Filmmaking and Video Production Career Tree, 126

Health Science Career Tree, 125

Manufacturing Career Tree, 153

Math Career Tree, 127

overview, 116, 117

Sports Medicine and Personal Training Career Tree, 128

Welding Career Tree, 129

Professional Skills, 16, 144–45

R

Raymond, Cathie, 53, 79–80, 158

respect, generational differences in perspective, 186–88

Root System (Career Tree), 142–47

academics, 143–44

experiences, 145–46

passion, 146–47

professional skills, 144–45

Rowe, Mike, 26

S

safety nets, danger of, 67–71

Salem-Keizer Public Schools, 133

Schottke, Jen, 80–81

self-esteem

building, 75

entitled mindset, 68–69

failure and, 75–76

self-motivation, 77–78. *See also* Light at the End of the Tunnel motivational strategy

The 7 Habits of Highly Effective People (Covey), 39

Shapiro & Duncan, Inc., 3

Silent Generation, 36

skills gap, 15–32

changing hiring strategies, 24–25

choosing level of education needed for career goals, 18–22

college and career ready concept, 19

CTE programs, 27–29

drug use and, 26–27

expectation and educational paradigm, 18–19

general discussion, 15–22

hard skills, 16

insights from Fortune 100 Executives, 22–29

Kevin Fleming's study of, 16–17

manufacturing industry, 23–26

1:2:7 ratio, 17

overview, 30–31

soft skills, 16

Sload, David, 68

Smith, Billie, 175

Snapchat, 46

social media, 46–47, 183–84

soft skills, 16, 144

Space Race, 9–10

Sports Medicine and Personal Training Career Tree, 127–28

Entry-Level Careers, 127–28

Professional Careers, 128

Technical Careers, 128

Sputnik, 9

stereotypes, about younger generations, 38

strategic planning stage (creaking-branch metaphor). *See also* Light at the End of the Tunnel motivational strategy; skills gap

defined, 1–2

overview, 11–12

strategies and tools. *See also* Career
Tree; Education with Purpose; Light
at the End of the Tunnel motivational strategy

   Career Tree best practices, 188–
96, 198

      activating entrepreneurs,
193–96

      career conversations, 192–93

      Career Plan of the Week
award, 189

      Career Tree Tuesdays, 189

      interactive wall graphic, 191

      keeping alumni engaged,
191–92

      networking roots, 190

      overview, 188

      Plan A career, 189–90

      Plan B career, 190

      Tree Week, 189

      YouTube It, 190–91

   challenges as, 180, 197

   expectations, 185–86, 197

   interactive relationships, 181–84,
197

   respect, 186–88

   structure, 181

   supportive education and work
environment, 180–81, 197

student loan debt, 18, 169–70

student-run enterprises, 194

"Success in the New Economy"
(video), 16–17

T

Technical Careers

   Art and Performing Arts Career
Tree, 122

Automotive Career Tree, 120

County Government and Law
Career Tree, 124

Education Career Tree, 123

Filmmaking and Video Production Career Tree, 126

Health Science Career Tree, 125

Manufacturing Career Tree, 153

Math Career Tree, 127

overview, 115, 117

Sports Medicine and Personal
Training Career Tree, 128

Welding Career Tree, 129

technology

   importance of interactive relationships to Why Generation,
181–84

   social media, 46–47, 183–84

   tech savvy, 50–51, 63

texting, generational differences in
style, 182–83

TFS company, 5–7, 61–62

tools. *See* strategies and tools

Tracy, Brian, 89–90

Tree Week, 189

"trophy kids", 68

Twitter, 46

U

"unique, special, and important" concept, 48–49, 63

university. *See* college; education

UPS (United Parcel Service), 56–57,
63

W

Wade Factor story, 199–210

"want-to," "how-to" concept, 94–101

   defined, 105

Nick's story, 95–101
overview, 94–95
Welcome Original Thinkers program
    (Kimberly-Clark company), 58
Welding Career Tree, 128–29
    Entry-Level Careers, 128–29
    Professional Careers, 129
    Technical Careers, 129
What's In It For Me? (WIIFM), 174
Why Generation
    butt-kissing approach of employ-
        ers, 57–60
    defined, 4–5
    entitled mindset, 51–57, 63
    experience-is-everything concept,
        45–47, 63
    focus of, 51
    Generational Rifts, 34–36, 38, 44
    group dynamic, 49–50
    importance of friends, 46
    loyalty in workplace, 60–61, 64
    multitasking, 55
    online presence, 46–47
    "open book" philosophy, 46

priorities of, 42–43, 45, 48–49
role of friends in life, 46
sense of individuality, 48–49
social media/online presence,
    46–47
team-oriented, 54
technology and, 50–51, 63,
    181–84
at TFS, 61–62
unique, special, and important
    concept, 48–49, 63
workplace expectations, 51–57
WIIFM (What's In It For Me?), 174
work-life blend, 41–43
workplace
    loyalty in, 60–61, 64
    workplace expectations, 51–57
"work to live" creed, 40–42
World War II, 9

Y

YouTube, as career exploration tool,
    190–91

About the Author

Mark C. Perna is the founder and CEO of TFS in Cleveland, Ohio, a full-service strategic communications and consulting firm whose mission is to share and support every client's passion for making a difference. Mark, a graduate of John Carroll University, has many years of experience addressing industry leaders on the topic of expanding their reach in an increasingly global marketplace. As an international expert on Generations Y and Z, Mark has devoted his career to empowering educators and employers to unleash the tremendous potential of today's young people, both in the classroom and on the job.

After successfully parenting two millennials as a single father, Mark has become a passionate advocate for bridging the generational divides that are contributing to America's profound skills gap. Parents, schools, districts, businesses, and state organizations of all sizes across North America have successfully used Mark's insights and strategies to connect more effectively with the younger generations. In his work with educational and business organizations, Mark has pioneered many best practices for achieving more with today's young people, including the TFS Education with Purpose®

philosophy and highly popular Career Tree® strategy, among others. Mark is frequently cited as the national expert in education enrollment, retention, and performance.

A dynamic and motivational public speaker, Mark frequently delivers keynote speeches at national and statewide events and spoke at Harvard University by special invitation. His genuine personality and warm sense of humor make him a fun and memorable communicator that people connect with immediately. He regularly addresses both small groups and massive crowds in his capacity as a generational and performance expert, reaching thousands of educators, employers, parents, and young people each year with his powerful message of change and empowerment. Mark has published numerous articles in national publications as a recognized voice in student engagement and success.

Mark enjoys inspirational movies, theater, travel, golf, wine, and time with his family—especially the latest Pernas, granddaughters Ellie and Lou Lou. He resides in Cleveland, Ohio. Find out more about Mark and his work at MarkCPerna.com.

You can also follow Mark on: